AF258976

Kingdom Musings

A Parent's Journal

60-Day Journey to Healing & Growth

CHRISTY COPELAND

Kingdom Musings

© 2025 by Christy Copeland

All rights reserved.

No part of this publication—whether in print, digital, or audio format—may be reproduced, distributed, or transmitted in any form or by any means, including photocopying, recording, or other electronic or mechanical methods, without the prior written permission of the publisher, except in the case of brief quotations used in critical reviews or other noncommercial purposes as permitted by copyright law.

For permission requests, write to the publisher at info@leaderswellnesssuite.com.
Published by Leaders Wellness Suite LLC Lockport, Illinois www.leaderswellnesssuite.com

Scripture quotations taken from The Holy Bible,
New International Version® NIV® Copyright © 1973, 1978, 1984, 2011 by Biblica, Inc.
Used with permission. All rights reserved worldwide.

Scripture quotations taken from the New King James Version®.
Copyright © 1982 by Thomas Nelson. Used by permission. All rights reserved.

Printed in the United States of America.

Print: 978-1-732-7171-4-5
Ebook: 978-1-732-7171-5-2

Category:
Religion / Christian Living / Family & Relationships

Note to the Reader:
This book is for informational purposes only.
Readers are encouraged to seek additional support from trusted mentors or professionals as needed.

Table of Contents

Preface

Thank you for joining me on this 60-day journey of reflection, healing, and growth. Let me be honest here—sometimes life doesn't go as planned. Many make it look so easy on social media, and it truly is beautiful to see. But behind the smiles and curated moments, there are often stories of struggle, pain, and triumph. My story is one of those.

As a divorced parent, I faced challenges that tested me deeply. I wanted to present my children with a hopeful view of life, even as I was working through my own brokenness. I knew that if I was to build them up, I had to lean into my faith, trusting God to help me stay positive and intentional. Healing is messy, and there were days when I felt far from capable, but I chose to keep showing up, trusting God's grace to fill in the gaps.

This journal is an invitation for you to walk through that same kind of journey—embracing both the struggles and the victories. Each day will focus on a different aspect of rebuilding after difficult times, whether you're recovering from loss, navigating a tough transition, or simply seeking a deeper connection with yourself and God. Through scripture, reflections, and moments of prayer, my hope is that you'll find encouragement, just as I did.

I know what it feels like to walk this road, and I also know what it feels like to come out on the other side, a little stronger, a little wiser, and filled with hope for the future. No matter where you are today, God has a plan for you, and it's good. Let's take this 60-day journey together, building as we heal and trusting that God's grace is more than enough for each day ahead.

The Hebrew word for "muse," hagah, is so much deeper than simply meditating. It invites us to worship, reflect, speak out loud, and praise. When we muse on Scripture, it's like taking the time to truly savor and enjoy it, letting it lead us into prayer, self-reflection, and heartfelt praise.

WEEK 1

Finding Peace in Chaos

Today I'm grateful for...

____

____

____

____

____

____

____

____

____

____

____

"You can be a courageous parent transforming with strength & dominion."
—Christy Copeland

A New Beginning

"See, I am doing a new thing! Now it springs up; do you not perceive it? I am making a way in the wilderness and streams in the wasteland."
— Isaiah 43:19

When we're burdened with painful emotions, it can feel like we're wandering through a wilderness with no end in sight. Grief, anger, and sorrow can cloud our vision, making it difficult to see beyond our current struggles. But God, in His infinite love and wisdom, invites us to lay down these burdens and trust in His promise of new beginnings.

Choosing to resolve our painful emotions is a courageous step. It means confronting our hurt, forgiving those who have wronged us, and ultimately, forgiving ourselves. It's about allowing God to heal our wounds and restore our broken hearts. This process is not easy, and it requires a deep reliance on God's strength and grace today.

As we embrace this journey of healing, we also open ourselves to the new seasons God has planned for us. Just as the seasons change in nature, bringing new life and renewal, God promises to bring transformation and growth into our lives. He is making a way in the wilderness and streams in the wasteland. This means that even in our most barren and desolate places, God is at work, creating pathways and bringing forth life.

God's scope is much larger than we can imagine. His plans for us are far beyond our understanding, encompassing not just our present circumstances, but a future filled with hope and promise. When we trust in God's bigness, we can release our fears and anxieties, knowing that He holds our lives in His hands.

So today, let's choose to resolve our painful emotions and embrace the new seasons God is bringing into our lives. Let's lean into His promise in Isaiah 43:19, believing that He is doing a new thing within us. Together, we can walk this path of faith, trusting that God is leading us toward a future filled with His love and grace.

Thank you for being here with me. I'm excited to see how God will move in our lives as we journey together.

Prayer

Heavenly Father, I come before You with a heart open to Your guidance and renewal. Thank You for Your promise of new beginnings. Help me to release the painful emotions and pressures that weigh me down. I trust in Your power to transform my life, making a way in the wilderness and bringing streams in the wasteland. Fill me with Your peace, strength, and hope as I step into this new season with You. In Jesus' name, Amen.

Faith in Action - A New Beginning

Take some quiet time today to journal about the areas in your life where you need a fresh start. Write down the painful emotions you're ready to release and the hopes you have for the new season God is preparing for you. Then, spend a few moments in prayer, asking God to guide you and fill you with His renewing spirit.

DAY 2

Embracing Stillness

"Be still, and know that I am God"
— Psalm 46:10

Raising four children while juggling the demands of a busy career, school activities, and the ever-present concern of housing and food insecurity was, at times, overwhelming. I remember countless nights of meal prepping for the week ahead, ensuring homework was done, and running late to attend the various school activities—all while trying to keep the home running smoothly. It often felt like I was on a never-ending treadmill, running at full speed but never quite catching up.

During those years, there was one verse that provided me with an anchor, a lifeline in the storm: "Be still, and know that I am God" (Psalm 46:10). This verse is a beautiful reminder that even in the busyness, we are invited to pause and recognize God's presence in our lives. It's a call to let go of our frantic efforts and trust in His divine plan.

Embracing stillness was not easy. It requires intentionality and faith. I began carving out moments of quiet despite the chaos. Sometimes it was a few minutes in the early morning before the children woke up, in my bedroom and reading a devotional. Other times, it was finding a peaceful corner during lunch breaks to breathe and pray. These small pockets of stillness became sacred, restoring my spirit and renewing my strength.

Through these moments, I learned that stillness is not about inactivity but about finding peace in God's presence. It's about trusting that He is in control, even when our world feels out of control. The act of being still allows us to reconnect with what truly matters and to hear the gentle whispers of God's guidance.

For those of you overcoming similar challenges—balancing the demands of family, work, and the uncertainties of life—I encourage you to embrace stillness. Start with just a few minutes each day. Find a quiet space, breathe deeply, and focus on God's promise in Psalm 46:10. Let go of your worries and allow His peace to wash over you.

Remember, it's in the stillness that we find clarity, strength, and the reassurance that we are not alone. God is with us, guiding us through every trial and triumph. So, take a moment today to be still and know that He is God. Let this truth settle in your heart and transform the way you move through the busyness of life.

Prayer

Heavenly Father,

Lord, You know the challenges we face—balancing work, family, and the constant concerns of our daily needs. We lift our burdens to You, trusting in Your promise to be our refuge and strength.

Teach us to embrace stillness, to pause and recognize Your presence in every moment. Help us to find those precious pockets of quiet where we can breathe deeply and rest in Your love. Remind us that we do not walk this journey alone; You are always with us, guiding and sustaining us. May we continually return to the truth of Psalm 46:10, knowing that You are God and You are in control.

In Jesus' name, we pray. Amen.

Faith in Action – Embracing Stillness

Reflect on a time when you were able to find moments of stillness and peace despite feeling overwhelmed by life's demands. What did you do to create those moments, and how did they positively impact your overall well-being and perspective?

____

____

____

Trusting God in Uncertainty

"Trust in the Lord with all your heart and lean not on your own understanding; in all your ways submit to him, and he will make your paths straight." — **Proverbs 3:5-6**

Imagine being a divorced parent, raising four beautiful children alone. Life is challenging, but you find strength and joy in your family. Then, tragedy strikes—one of your children suffers a serious accident, leading to years of recovery. The weight of worry, fear, and uncertainty feels overwhelming.

In moments like these, it's easy to question everything. Why did this happen? How will we get through this? But it's in these darkest times that Proverbs 3:5-6 becomes our lifeline. Trusting in God means surrendering our fears and uncertainties to Him, believing that He will guide us through even the most challenging paths.

During my own journey, I found that when I leaned on God's understanding instead of my own, He provided unexpected support and strength. Whether it was through a kind word from a friend, a moment of peace in prayer, or the resilience of my children, God's presence was evident.

Each day, I made a conscious choice to trust Him. I prayed for wisdom and patience, and gradually, I saw His hand in our healing process. The road was long and often difficult, but God's guidance never wavered. He provided for our needs, opened doors for medical care, and surrounded us with a community of love and support.

If you are facing similar struggles, I encourage you to hold onto Proverbs 3:5-6. Trust in the Lord with all your heart, even when the path is uncertain. Lean not on your own understanding, but submit to Him. He will make your paths straight, bringing peace and hope in His perfect time.

At Leaders Wellness Suite, we walk this journey together, supporting and uplifting one another through faith and love. You are not alone. Trust in God, and let Him guide you through the uncertainty to brighter days ahead.

Prayer

Father God, we come before You with humble hearts, acknowledging our need for Your guidance and grace. Lord, You know the areas of our lives where we struggle to let go and trust in Your plan. Help us to release our fears and anxieties into Your loving hands. Strengthen our faith so that we may trust You more deeply, especially in the midst of uncertainty. May Your peace, which surpasses all understanding, guard our hearts and minds. We ask for Your wisdom and direction in every decision we make. Thank You for Your unwavering love and faithfulness. In Jesus' name, we pray. Amen.

Faith in Action - Trusting God in Uncertainty

Take a few moments today to identify one specific area of your life where you find it difficult to trust God fully. Write it down and commit it to prayer, asking God to help you surrender this part of your life to Him. Then, take a tangible step towards trust—whether it's through seeking counsel, joining a support group, or simply letting go of a worry you've been holding onto. Trust that God is with you, guiding your path.

____

____

____

____

____

Restoring Hope After Loss

"May the God of hope fill you with all joy and peace as you trust in him, so that you may overflow with hope by the power of the Holy Spirit."
— Romans 15:13

Whether it's the loss of a loved one, the end of a significant relationship, or any other form of deep emotional pain, rebuilding our households and our hearts can seem dreadful. However, God's promise in Romans 15:13 reminds us that we can find joy, peace, and an overflowing hope through Him.

The pain of loss can leave us feeling empty, overwhelmed, and unsure of how to move forward. In these moments, it's essential to remember that we are not alone. God, our source of hope, is ever-present and ready to fill us with His joy and peace. This doesn't mean we won't grieve or feel sorrow, but it does mean that in the midst of our pain, we can experience God's comforting presence.

Take a moment today to pause and breathe in God's peace. Allow yourself to feel His embrace and the promise that joy and peace are possible, even now.

Trusting God during times of loss can be challenging, but it is through this trust that we can begin to see His plans for our lives unfold. Romans 15:13 encourages us to place our trust in Him so that we may be filled with hope. This hope is not a superficial optimism, but a deep-seated assurance that God is in control and has a purpose for our pain.

Reflect on the ways God has been present in your life before. How has He provided, comforted, and guided you? Use these reflections as stepping stones to build your trust in His plan for your future.

As we lean into God's faithfulness, we begin to overflow with hope. This hope is not generated by our own efforts but by the power of the Holy Spirit working within us. He empowers us to rebuild our households and lives on a foundation that cannot be shaken, no matter what storms come our way.

Prayer

Heavenly Father, we come before You today, seeking Your comfort and hope. Thank You for the promise in Romans 15:13 that You will fill us with all joy and peace as we trust in You. Help us to place our faith in Your plans, even when we don't understand them. Fill us with the power of Your Holy Spirit, so that we may overflow with hope and rebuild our households on a foundation of Your love and grace. In Jesus' name, Amen.

Faith in Action - Restoring Hope After Loss

Take time today to create a small space in your home dedicated to prayer and reflection. Fill it with items that bring you comfort and remind you of God's promises. Use this space to meet with God daily, seeking His joy, peace, and hope as you rebuild your life.

____

____

____

____

____

Strength in Weakness

"But he said to me, 'My grace is sufficient for you, for my power is made perfect in weakness.' Therefore, I will boast all the more gladly of my weaknesses, so that the power of Christ may rest upon me."
— 2 Corinthians 12:9 (NKJV)

As we travel along the path of rebuilding and leading our families, we often confront our own limitations—those moments where we feel inadequate or overwhelmed by all that is on our shoulders. These moments can leave us feeling like we're not enough, or that we're failing to meet the needs of those depending on us. Yet, God's promise in 2 Corinthians 12:9 reminds us that His strength is greatest exactly where we feel weakest. He doesn't require perfection from us; He simply asks us to trust Him in our imperfections.

When we bring our weaknesses to God, we invite His power to work in ways beyond our natural ability. Our weaknesses, in God's hands, become a gateway to His strength. When we lean into this truth, we find freedom from the pressure of doing it all on our own. We're reminded that our role isn't about having all the answers or never making mistakes; it's about relying on God's grace in every season. Our families don't need a perfect leader—they need one who trusts God in all things.

Embracing our weaknesses isn't easy. It requires humility and the courage to let go of the illusion of control. Yet, in acknowledging where we fall short, we can rest in God's sufficiency. His strength fills in our gaps, and His grace covers us when we feel we're not enough. This surrender isn't a sign of failure but of wisdom, as we recognize that God is the ultimate source of strength for ourselves and our families.

As you lead your family, reflect on the areas where you feel least confident. Ask God to fill those places with His strength. Trust that He is faithful to equip you, not necessarily by removing your weaknesses, but by empowering you through them. Each moment of reliance on God becomes an opportunity to model faith and trust for your family, showing them that true strength comes from leaning on the Lord.

Prayer

Heavenly Father, thank You for Your grace that meets me right where I am, in every weakness and every doubt. Help me to surrender my insecurities to You, trusting that You will be my strength and my guide. Today, I commit to letting go of the pressure to do it all perfectly. Strengthen me to lead my family with humility and faith, knowing that Your power rests on me.

Faith in Action - Strength in Weakness

Take a few moments to list the areas where you feel weakest or most overwhelmed. Pray over each one, releasing them to God, and ask for His strength to work through you. Trust that, as you surrender, He will empower you with all you need for each day.

____

____

____

____

Overcoming Anxious Thoughts

"Do not be anxious about anything, but in every situation, by prayer and petition, with thanksgiving, present your requests to God. And the peace of God, which transcends all understanding, will guard your hearts and your minds in Christ Jesus." — **Philippians 4:6-7**

Whether you're adjusting to single parenting, searching for a safer place to live, or finding reliable child care, Philippians 4:6-7 offers us a profound promise of peace that can transform our lives even in the midst of anxiety and transition.

Reflect on how anxiety manifests in your life. What specific responsibilities or future concerns tend to overwhelm you? How does this anxiety affect your daily life and your relationship with God? This passage reminds us that through prayer and petition, paired with a heart of thanksgiving, we can present our concerns to God. This act of surrender allows His peace to guard our hearts and minds.

Consider the power of prayer in shifting your focus from worry to trust. When you bring your anxieties before God, you acknowledge His sovereignty and seek His guidance. Thanksgiving, even in the midst of uncertainty, realigns your perspective, helping you to see God's faithfulness and provision.

Prayer

Heavenly Father, I come before You with the anxieties that weigh heavily on my heart. As a divorced parent, I am often overwhelmed by responsibilities and uncertainties about the future. Your Word assures me that I do not need to be anxious but to bring all my concerns to You through prayer and thanksgiving. Lord, help me to release my worries to You, trusting in Your wisdom and provision. I commit to creating a prayer list of the specific anxieties I face. Each day, I will lift these concerns to You, acknowledging Your power and grace in every situation. Fill my heart with Your peace, which transcends all understanding, and guard my mind from the fears that seek to overwhelm me. I trust that Your peace will envelop me as I place my trust in Your care. Help me to cultivate a spirit of thanksgiving, recognizing Your continual presence and support in my life. In Jesus' name, Amen.

Faith in Action – Overcoming Anxious Thoughts

Today, take a few moments to write down your anxious thoughts and present them to God in prayer. Then, list three things you are grateful for and thank God for these blessings. Consider reaching out to a trusted friend, family member, or community resource for support as you move through your journey of healing and rebuilding.

____

____

____

____

Reflect and Recharge on Peace in Chaos

"Peace I leave with you; my peace I give you. I do not give to you as the world gives. Do not let your hearts be troubled and do not be afraid."
— John 14:27

Thank you for joining me on this journey of exploring peace in the midst of chaos. Over the past few days, we have delved into understanding how to find calm and serenity even when life feels overwhelming. Today, let's take a moment to reflect and recharge, allowing God's peace to renew our hearts and minds.

Reflect & Recharge

Think back on the devotionals we've shared about finding peace. We learned that true peace doesn't come from our circumstances but from our relationship with Jesus. It's a peace that surpasses all understanding and guards our hearts and minds (Philippians 4:7).

Consider the moments this past week where you felt God's peace. Were there specific scriptures, prayers, or actions that helped you connect with His calming presence? How did these practices shift your perspective amidst the chaos?

As we reflect on these lessons, let's focus on recharging our spirits. Here are some practical steps to help you maintain and deepen your sense of peace:

☐ Daily Connection with God: Set aside time each day to pray, read scripture, and listen for God's voice. His presence is a constant source of peace.

- ☐ Gratitude Journaling: Keep a journal where you write down things you are grateful for each day. Gratitude shifts our focus from problems to blessings, fostering a peaceful heart.
- ☐ Scripture Meditation: Choose a peace-related scripture to meditate on throughout the week. Let its truth anchor your thoughts and calm your spirit.

Prayer

Heavenly Father, thank You for the precious gift of Your peace. In a world full of chaos, Your peace is our sanctuary. Help us to remember that Your peace is not dependent on our circumstances but on Your unchanging presence. As we reflect on what we've learned, may Your peace continue to guard our hearts and minds. Teach us to draw closer to You each day, finding rest in Your promises. We trust in Your ability to calm every storm in our lives. In Jesus' name, Amen.

Faith in Action - Reflect and Recharge on Peace in the Midst of Chaos

Take some quiet time today to reflect on the peace you've experienced over the past week. Write down any moments where you felt God's peace, and thank Him for these blessings. Commit to one or more of the practical steps listed above to help you maintain this peace in the coming days.

____

____

____

____

____

This Week's Goals

Specific — What am I led to accomplish and why?
Measurable — How will I know when I have accomplished it?
Achievable — How can I accomplish this goal?
Relevant — Is this the right time for me to be working towards this goal?
Timebound — When do I want to accomplish this goal by?

☑ *Goal 1*

____

____

____

____

☑ *Goal 2*

____

____

____

____

☑ *Goal 3*

____

____

____

____

WEEK 2

Healing from Past Wounds

Today I'm grateful for...

____

____

____

____

____

____

____

____

____

____

____

____

"You can be a courageous parent transforming with strength & dominion."
—Christy Copeland

Courage to Confront Painful Emotions

"The Lord is close to the brokenhearted and saves those who are crushed in spirit." — **Psalm 34:18**

Rebuilding our households after significant changes or trauma can bring up a whirlwind of emotions. Fear and broken expectations often rise to the surface, making it difficult to move forward. It's natural to feel overwhelmed by these emotions, but God promises that He is near to the brokenhearted.

Psalm 34:18 reassures us that the Lord is not distant; He is intimately aware of our struggles and stands ready to save us. This truth gives us the courage to confront our painful emotions, knowing we are not alone in our journey.

As we move forward, let's hold onto the truth of Psalm 34:18. God is close to us in our brokenness and ready to save us. With His presence, we can find the courage to confront our painful emotions and rebuild our households on the foundation of His unwavering love and faithfulness.

Prayer

Heavenly Father, I come to You with my broken heart, filled with fear and disappointment. Thank You for Your promise in Psalm 34:18 that You are close to the brokenhearted and save those who are crushed in spirit. Help me to confront my painful emotions with courage, knowing that You are with me every step of the way. Surround me with Your love and the support of a caring community. Heal my heart and guide me as I rebuild my household. In Jesus' name, Amen.

Faith in Action - Courage to Confront Painful Emotions

Today, take a moment to write down your fears and disappointments. Present these emotions to God in prayer, acknowledging His presence with you. Then, join the Parent Power Pact to share your journey and receive our support. Finally, identify one small step you can take today towards rebuilding your household and celebrate that step as a victory.

Forgiveness and Freedom

"Get rid of all bitterness, rage and anger, brawling and slander, along with every form of malice. Be kind and compassionate to one another, forgiving each other, just as in Christ God forgave you." — **Ephesians 4:31-32**

Today, we will explore the liberating power of forgiveness and the freedom that comes from releasing others from our assumptions of justice as we work to rebuild our households. Ephesians 4:31-32 reminds us to let go of negative emotions and embrace kindness, compassion, and forgiveness, just as God forgave us through Christ.

Rebuilding our households after trauma or conflict often involves confronting deep-seated hurts and grievances. It's natural to hold onto feelings of anger, bitterness, and a desire for justice. We may feel that those who hurt us deserve to face the consequences of their actions. However, holding others to our assumptions of justice can become a heavy burden that impedes our healing and growth.

Ephesians 4:31-32 calls us to a higher standard of living, one that mirrors the grace and forgiveness God has shown us. By letting go of bitterness, rage, and anger, we free ourselves from the chains of resentment. Forgiving others does not mean that we condone their actions; rather, it means that we release them from our judgment and entrust them to God's perfect justice and mercy.

Forgiveness is a powerful act of faith. It requires us to trust that God's justice is better than our own and to believe that His grace can transform even the most painful situations. As we forgive, we open our hearts to healing and allow God's love to flow through us, bringing peace and restoration to our households.

Prayer

Heavenly Father, thank You for Your incredible grace and forgiveness. Help me to release any bitterness, anger, and desire for justice that I am holding onto. Teach me to forgive others as You have forgiven me, and to trust in Your perfect justice. Fill my heart with kindness and compassion, and let Your love flow through me as I rebuild my household. In Jesus' name, Amen.

Faith in Action – Forgiveness and Freedom

Today, take a moment to write down the names of those you need to forgive. Bring this list to God in prayer, asking Him to help you release these individuals from your judgment and entrust them to His care.

____

____

____

____

DAY 10

Healing Through Community

"Carry each other's burdens, and in this way you will fulfill the law of Christ." — **Galatians 6:2**

Today, we will explore the importance of healing through a supportive community, such as The Parent Power Pact, as we rebuild our households. Galatians 6:2 reminds us to carry each other's burdens, fulfilling the law of Christ through love and support.

Rebuilding our households after significant changes or trauma can feel overwhelming and isolating. During such times, the support of a caring community is invaluable. Healing through a community like the Parent Power Pact provides a sense of belonging, understanding, and shared strength.

Being part of a community where you can express yourself freely and receive understanding without fear of judgment is crucial for healing and growth. This sense of safety allows us to share our burdens, receive encouragement, and offer support to others in return.

Galatians 6:2 calls us to carry each other's burdens, emphasizing the mutual support and compassion that should characterize our relationships. By healing through a community and fostering a trusting and understanding environment, we can overcome the challenges of rebuilding our households with greater resilience and hope.

Prayer

Heavenly Father, thank You for the gift of community and the support it provides. Help me to heal through my community and find strength as I rebuild my household.

Teach me to carry others' burdens with love and compassion, fulfilling the law of Christ. Guide our community to be a place of trust, understanding, and mutual support. Surround us with Your love and grace, and help us to grow together in strength and faith. In Jesus' name, Amen.

Faith in Action – Healing through Community

Today, take a moment to connect with your community. Share a piece of your journey with someone you trust, and offer your support to someone in need. Reflect on how you can contribute to creating a safe and supportive environment within your community. Remember, healing through each other's support and carrying each other's burdens is a powerful way to fulfill the law of Christ.

God's Unfailing Love

"For I am convinced that neither death nor life, neither angels nor demons, neither the present nor the future, nor any powers, neither height nor depth, nor anything else in all creation, will be able to separate us from the love of God that is in Christ Jesus our Lord." — **Romans 8:38-39**

Today, we will explore the unfailing love of God, especially as we face judgment from ourselves and others after experiencing loss and as we work to rebuild our households. Romans 8:38-39 assures us that nothing can separate us from the love of God in Christ Jesus.

Loss can bring a torrent of emotions—grief, sadness, and even self-judgment or judgment from others. During these times, it's easy to feel isolated and unworthy. We might question our decisions, blame ourselves for circumstances beyond our control, or feel the weight of others' criticisms.

In these moments, it's essential to remember God's unfailing love. Romans 8:38-39 declares that nothing in all creation can separate us from the love of God. His love is constant and unchanging, regardless of our circumstances or the judgments we face. Embracing this truth provides the comfort and strength we need to heal and rebuild.

As we rebuild our households, we must hold on to this promise of God's unbreakable love. It is His love that lifts us, sustains us, and empowers us to overcome the challenges we face.

Prayer

Heavenly Father, thank You for Your unfailing love that nothing can separate us from. Help me to embrace this truth and find comfort in Your constant love, especially when facing self-judgment or judgment from others. Guide me as I rebuild my household, and remind me daily of Your grace and acceptance. Surround me with Your love and strengthen me with Your peace. In Jesus' name, Amen.

Faith in Action – God's Unfailing Love

Today, take a moment to write down Romans 8:38-39 and place it somewhere visible. Whenever you feel overwhelmed by judgment or self-criticism, read these verses and remind yourself of God's unwavering love. Reflect on His promises and allow them to uplift and strengthen you as you continue to rebuild your household.

____

____

____

____

____

Finding Your Breath Again: Rest in God's Presence

"But those who wait on the Lord Shall renew their strength; They shall mount up with wings like eagles, They shall run and not be weary, They shall walk and not faint." — **Isaiah 40:31**

If you've ever found yourself holding your breath, tightening your chest as if your body's on high alert, you're not alone. Trauma, anxiety, or the feeling of wanting to disappear because of shame can have us instinctively restricting the very thing that gives us life: our breath. I even discovered during my marathon training that my shallow breathing was limiting my ability to run long distances. This silent habit can keep us in survival mode, holding on to tension, even long after the original stress or shame is gone. Today, let's talk about the gift of diaphragmatic breathing and finding rest in God's presence.

The Weight of Unspoken Pain

Shame often makes our bodies feel like they aren't our own. Anxiety keeps our minds busy—preoccupied with past regrets or future fears—making it easy to forget the most natural, God-given rhythm of all: breathing. I remember seasons when I'd catch myself barely inhaling, my body clinging to stress as if exhaling would mean losing control. Perhaps you've experienced this too. You see, when our souls carry unspoken pain, our bodies respond, tightening, bracing for danger. It's a way of saying, "I'm not ready. I'm not safe."

The tricky part is that this restricted way of breathing can become a habit, even if the original stimulus—the trauma, the anxiety, the shame—is no longer present. The body remembers the posture of fear, and before we know it, shallow breathing becomes our new normal. But our Father never designed us to carry life's weight without His help. He didn't create us to feel like we have to disappear because of shame. He gave us His Spirit, His breath, as proof that we matter. And this breath can bring us to a place of rest, a place of being held by Him.

Diaphragmatic Breathing: A Gentle Rescue

Diaphragmatic breathing, often called "belly breathing," is a beautiful way to calm the body and reconnect with the safety found in God. It invites us to take a moment to simply be still, to be present. When we breathe deeply, filling our lungs until our bellies expand, we are giving ourselves a reminder that we are safe, that we are not alone in this journey. Each deep breath invites God's peace to replace our anxiety, His presence to fill the emptiness of shame.

A Practice to Ground Us in Him

Find a quiet moment, place your hand on your belly, and inhale deeply through your nose, filling your lungs until you feel your belly rise. Hold for just a second, then slowly exhale through your mouth, releasing any tension. With every inhale, imagine God's peace filling you. With every exhale, let go of anxiety and the feeling of wanting to disappear because of shame. As we take these breaths, we are reminded that our breath, our life, is a gift from God. And each one brings us back to Him. Just like Isaiah says, our hope in God renews our strength. Through His presence, we can soar, run without growing weary, and walk without fainting.

Prayer

Heavenly Father, thank You for the breath You have given me. Help me to find rest in You, to slow down, to be still, and to know that You are the One who renews my strength. I release the anxieties and fears that keep me from fully breathing in Your peace. Let every breath I take remind me of Your presence and Your promise to sustain me. In Jesus' name, Amen.

Faith in Action – Finding Your Breath Again: Rest in God's Presence

This week, take time to practice diaphragmatic breathing, especially in moments when you feel anxious or disconnected. Find a verse like Isaiah 40:31, and as you breathe deeply, let the words echo in your heart. Allow God's peace to wash over you, breath by breath.

Rebuilding Trust

"And those who know Your name will put their trust in You; For You, Lord, have not forsaken those who seek You." — **Psalms 9:10**

Today, we will reflect on the importance of rebuilding trust in our households, drawing strength and guidance from Psalm 9:10. This verse reassures us that those who know God's name trust in Him, for He has never forsaken those who seek Him.

Rebuilding trust after a period of chaos or betrayal is a challenging but vital part of healing and restoring our households. Trust is the foundation of any healthy relationship, and without it, we can feel insecure and disconnected. Psalm 9:10 reminds us that our ultimate source of trust is in the Lord, who has never forsaken those who seek Him.

As we seek to rebuild trust within our households, it's important to remember that trust is not only given but also earned. It requires consistent effort, honesty, and patience from all involved. By grounding ourselves in God's unwavering trustworthiness, we can find the strength and guidance needed to restore trust in our relationships.

God's faithfulness serves as a perfect model for us. He is always reliable, steadfast, and true. When we seek Him and lean on His example, we can begin to rebuild trust with those around us, fostering an environment of security and love.

Prayer

Heavenly Father, thank You for being a God who is always trustworthy and faithful. Help me to rebuild trust within my household, drawing on Your example of steadfastness and love. Guide me to be honest, transparent, and reliable in all moments of vunerability.

Grant me patience and wisdom as I work to restore trust with those around me. May Your presence fill our home with security and peace. In Jesus' name, Amen.

Faith in Action - Rebuilding Trust

Today, take a moment to reflect on areas in your household where trust needs to be rebuilt. Identify specific actions you can take to foster trust and commit to making those changes. Pray for God's guidance and strength, and seek opportunities to demonstrate trustworthiness in your daily interactions.

____

____

____

____

____

DAY 14

Reflect and Recharge on Healing Past Wounds

"He heals the brokenhearted and binds up their wounds."
— Psalm 147:3

Thank you for joining me on this journey. This week, we have delved into the profound and necessary topic of healing past wounds. Let's take this time to reflect on what we've learned and recharge our spirits, grounded in the truth of God's word and His unfailing love.

Reflect & Recharge

Healing past wounds is a journey that requires us to confront our pain, seek God's comfort, and embrace His healing. Throughout this week, we have explored various aspects of this process—acknowledging our hurts, letting go of guilt, forgiving ourselves and others, and leaning into God's love and the support of our community.

Psalm 147:3 reassures us that God heals the brokenhearted and binds up their wounds. This promise is a beacon of hope, reminding us that no matter how deep our pain, God's love is deeper. He is intimately aware of our struggles and is always ready to bring healing to our lives.

As we reflect on this week's discussions, let's consider how we can apply these insights to our daily lives. Healing is a continual process that requires patience, faith, and intentionality. By staying close to God and drawing strength from His word and His people, we can experience profound restoration and peace.

Prayer

Heavenly Father, thank You for being the healer of our hearts. As we reflect on this week's journey of healing past wounds, we ask for Your continued guidance and comfort. Bind up our wounds and restore us with Your love. Help us to embrace Your promises and find strength in Your presence. Surround us with a supportive community and fill us with Your peace. In Jesus' name, Amen.

Faith in Action – Reflect and Recharge on Healing from Past Wounds

Today, take a few moments to write a letter to God about your healing journey. Share your struggles, your progress, and your hopes. Thank Him for His faithfulness and ask for His continued help. Keep this letter as a testament to His work in your life and as a reminder of His promises.

____

____

____

____

____

This Week's Goals

Specific — What am I led to accomplish and why?
Measurable — How will I know when I have accomplished it?
Achievable — How can I accomplish this goal?
Relevant — Is this the right time for me to be working towards this goal?
Timebound — When do I want to accomplish this goal by?

☑ *Goal 1*

____

____

____

____

☑ *Goal 2*

____

____

____

____

☑ *Goal 3*

____

____

____

____

WEEK 3

Strengthening Faith

Today I'm grateful for...

____

____

____

____

____

____

____

____

____

____

____

"You can be a courageous parent transforming with strength & dominion."
—Christy Copeland

Walking by Faith

"For we walk by faith, not by sight."
— **2 Corinthians 5:7**

Today, we will focus on the importance of taking the next steps on our journey, even when the way forward isn't entirely clear. 2 Corinthians 5:7 reminds us that we walk by faith, not by sight, encouraging us to trust in God's guidance and take courageous steps forward.

Every journey, especially one that involves rebuilding our households and healing from past wounds, requires us to take steps forward. Sometimes these steps can feel intimidating, especially when we don't know what lies ahead. It's in these moments that we must remember the powerful truth found in 2 Corinthians 5:7: "For we walk by faith, not by sight."

Walking by faith means trusting in God's plan and His timing, even when we cannot see the entire path before us. It involves stepping out in faith, believing that God is with us and will guide our steps. This trust allows us to move forward with confidence, knowing that God's presence is our constant companion.

As we consider the next steps in our journey, let's reflect on how we can walk by faith. Whether it's making a significant decision, stepping into a new role, or simply continuing our daily responsibilities, God calls us to trust Him and take those steps with courage and faith.

Prayer

Heavenly Father, thank You for being our guide and companion on this journey. Help us to walk by faith and not by sight, trusting in Your plan and timing. Give us the courage to take the next steps, even when the way forward is unclear. Surround us with Your peace and assurance, and strengthen our faith in Your promises. In Jesus' name, Amen.

Faith in Action - Walking by Faith

Identify one step you can take on your journey that requires faith. This could be a decision you need to make, a conversation you need to have, or an action you need to take. Bring this step before God in prayer, asking for His guidance and courage. Trust Him to lead you as you move forward.

____

____

____

____

God's Promises

*"Not one of all the Lord's good promises to Israel failed;
every one was fulfilled."* — **Joshua 21:45**

Today, we will reflect on the reliability of God's promises and celebrate the milestones achieved by our children as evidence of His faithfulness. Joshua 21:45 reminds us that not one of God's promises failed to Israel; every single one was fulfilled.

As parents, we hold countless hopes and dreams for our children. We pray for their growth, success, and happiness, trusting in God's promises to guide and protect them. Raising children who have become college graduates and now live independently is a profound testament to God's faithfulness and the power of His promises.

Joshua 21:45 is a powerful reminder that God is steadfast in His promises. Just as He fulfilled every promise to Israel, He fulfills His promises to us today. Reflecting on this truth, we can see how God's hand has been at work in our lives and the lives of our children.

Years ago, God gave me 11 keys for positive parenting, and I clung to those principles with faith. Through challenges and triumphs, these keys guided my parenting journey. Today, seeing my children continue to grow as independent adults is a testament to God's faithfulness and the fulfillment of His promises.

Prayer

Heavenly Father, thank You for Your unwavering faithfulness and the fulfillment of Your promises. As I reflect on Joshua 21:45, I am reminded of how You have guided and blessed my child(ren), helping them achieve their goals and live independently. Thank You for the principles of parenting and for Your presence in every step of our journey. Help me to continue trusting in Your promises and celebrating Your faithfulness. In Jesus' name, Amen.

Faith in Action - God's Promises

Today, take a moment to write a letter of gratitude to God. Reflect on the milestones your children have achieved and the ways you have seen God's promises fulfilled in your life. Share this letter with your children, celebrating God's faithfulness together and encouraging them to trust in His promises for their own journeys.

____

____

____

____

____

Faith in the Midst of Trials

"Consider it pure joy, my brothers and sisters, whenever you face trials of many kinds, because you know that the testing of your faith produces perseverance. Let perseverance finish its work so that you may be mature and complete, not lacking anything." — **James 1:2-4**

Today, let's take a closer look at maintaining faith in the midst of trials, especially when we find ourselves with not enough or just enough. James 1:2-4 encourages us to consider it pure joy when we face trials, knowing that these challenges test our faith and produce perseverance.

Life's trials can be rough, especially when we're rebuilding our households and resources seem scarce. Whether it's financial strain, emotional stress, or physical exhaustion, the feeling of having not enough or just enough can be overwhelming. Yet, James 1:2-4 invites us to view these trials from a different perspective—one of joy and growth.

James tells us that the testing of our faith through trials produces perseverance. This perseverance is essential for our spiritual maturity, making us complete and lacking nothing. It's a profound reminder that God uses our struggles to strengthen our faith and build our character.

As we face the trials of rebuilding our households, let's remember that God is at work in the midst of our challenges. He sees our needs and is faithful to provide for us, often in ways we may not expect. By trusting in Him and persevering through our difficulties, we can emerge stronger and more resilient.

Prayer

Heavenly Father, thank You for Your presence in the midst of our trials. Help us to view our challenges with joy, knowing that they are opportunities for our faith to grow. Strengthen us to persevere through difficulties and to trust in Your provision. As we rebuild our households, remind us that You are faithful and will supply our needs. In Jesus' name, Amen.

Faith in Action – Faith in the Midst of Trials

Take a moment to reflect on a challenging situation you are currently facing or have faced in the past. How has your faith been tested during this time? Consider how you've seen God's hand at work, even in the midst of difficulty.

____

____

____

____

____

Spiritual Disciplines

"For physical training is of some value, but godliness has value for all things, holding promise for both the present life and the life to come."
— 1 Timothy 4:8

Thank you for joining me on this journey. Today, we will focus on the importance of spiritual disciplines as we rebuild our households. 1 Timothy 4:8 reminds us that while physical training has some value, training in godliness is valuable in every aspect, holding promise for this life and the life to come.

Rebuilding our households after a significant change or loss requires not only practical adjustments but also a strong spiritual foundation. Just as athletes train their bodies for peak performance, we must also train our spirits to navigate life's challenges with grace and strength. Spiritual disciplines—such as prayer, Bible study, worship, and service—are essential practices that help us grow in godliness and resilience.

1 Timothy 4:8 emphasizes that godliness has value for all things. When we commit to spiritual disciplines, we invite God's presence and guidance into our daily lives. This spiritual training equips us to handle the complexities of rebuilding our households, fostering a sense of peace and direction that transcends our circumstances.

Prayer

Heavenly Father, thank You for the gift of spiritual disciplines that help us grow in godliness and resilience. As we rebuild our households, guide us to commit to practices that strengthen our relationship with You. Help us to find joy and peace in prayer,

Bible study, worship, service, and community. Equip us with Your wisdom and presence, so we may navigate this season with grace and faith. In Jesus' name, Amen.

Faith in Action – Spiritual Disciplines

Today, choose one spiritual discipline to focus on and integrate it into your daily routine. Whether it's setting aside time for prayer, starting a new Bible study plan, or finding a way to serve others, commit to this practice and invite God to work through it in your life.

____

____

____

____

____

God's Faithfulness

"Because of the Lord's great love we are not consumed, for His compassions never fail. They are new every morning; great is Your faithfulness."
— Lamentations 3:22-23

Today, let's celebrate the faithfulness of God as we get emotionally stronger. Lamentations 3:22-23 reminds us of God's great love and unfailing compassion, which are new every morning. Truly, great is His faithfulness.

Rebuilding our emotional strength can be a challenging process, especially when faced with the ups and downs of life. However, Lamentations 3:22-23 offers a profound reminder of God's unwavering faithfulness. His great love ensures that we are not consumed by our struggles, and His compassion renews us each day.

As we strive to become emotionally stronger, it's crucial to focus on God's faithfulness. Reflecting on His constant love and fresh mercies can provide the emotional resilience we need to navigate difficult times. Each new day is an opportunity to experience His grace and to grow in emotional strength, knowing that His compassion never fails.

Consider how God has sustained you through past difficulties and how His faithfulness has been a source of strength. By focusing on His unchanging nature, we can find the courage to face our emotional challenges and emerge stronger.

Prayer

Heavenly Father, thank You for Your great love and unfailing compassion. As we reflect on Lamentations 3:22-23, we are reminded that Your mercies are new every morning and that Your faithfulness is great. Help us to see Your hand in our lives as we work to become emotionally stronger. Give us hearts of gratitude and trust in Your ongoing provision and care. Strengthen us with Your presence, and help us to rely on Your steadfast love. In Jesus' name, Amen.

Faith in Action - God's faithfulness

Today, take a moment to write down three ways you have seen God's faithfulness in your life recently. Reflect on these instances and thank God for His ongoing love and compassion. Additionally, commit to a daily practice of acknowledging God's new mercies each morning, allowing His love to strengthen you emotionally.

____

____

____

____

____

Renewing Your Mind

"Do not conform to the pattern of this world, but be transformed by the renewing of your mind. Then you will be able to test and approve what God's will is—His good, pleasing and perfect will."
— Romans 12:2

Today, let's explore the importance of mind renewal and replacing old thought patterns with God's truth, as guided by Romans 12:2.

Our minds are powerful, shaping our perceptions, attitudes, and actions. Romans 12:2 urges us not to conform to the patterns of this world but to be transformed by the renewing of our minds. This transformation involves replacing old, unproductive thought patterns with new ones that align with God's will.

Old thought patterns often include negative self-talk, doubt, fear, and worldly influences that lead us away from God's truth. Mind renewal is an intentional process of identifying these harmful patterns and replacing them with thoughts that reflect God's promises and love.

Consider how your current thought patterns affect your daily life. Are there areas where you feel stuck or discouraged? Reflect on how God's truth can bring transformation and freedom. By continually renewing our minds with Scripture and prayer, we open ourselves to God's good, pleasing, and perfect will.

Prayer

Heavenly Father, thank You for the gift of transformation through the renewing of our minds. Help us to identify and release old thought patterns that do not align with

Your truth. Fill our minds with Your Word and guide us in understanding Your will. As we replace negative thoughts with Your promises, may we experience true transformation and a deeper sense of Your presence. In Jesus' name, Amen.

Faith in Action - Renewing Your Mind

Today, take a moment to identify one negative thought pattern that you frequently encounter. Write it down and then find a corresponding Scripture that speaks God's truth into that area. For example, if you struggle with fear, meditate on 2 Timothy 1:7: "For God has not given us a spirit of fear, but of power and of love and of a sound mind."

____

____

____

____

____

Reflect and Recharge on Strengthening Faith

"Now faith is confidence in what we hope for and assurance about what we do not see." — **Hebrews 11:1**

As we come to the end of the week, let's take some time to reflect and recharge on our topic of strengthening faith. Our anchor verse, Hebrews 11:1, reminds us that faith is about confidence in what we hope for and assurance in what we do not see.

Reflect & Recharge

This week, we've explored various aspects of strengthening our faith, recognizing that it's an ongoing journey filled with both challenges and triumphs. Faith involves trusting God's promises even when circumstances seem uncertain. It requires us to look beyond what we can see and believe in His steadfast love and faithfulness.

Reflect on the moments this week when you felt your faith being tested. How did you respond? Did you turn to God's Word for reassurance? Did you seek His presence in prayer? Strengthening our faith means consistently turning to God, trusting in His plan, and finding assurance in His promises.

Consider how the lessons and reflections from this week have impacted your faith journey. What has God revealed to you about His faithfulness and your ability to trust Him more deeply?

Prayer

Heavenly Father, thank You for guiding us through this week as we focused on strengthening our faith. We are grateful for the ways You've spoken to our hearts and drawn us closer to You. Help us to hold onto the confidence and assurance that comes from faith in You. Continue to strengthen our trust in Your promises and remind us that You are always with us, even when we cannot see the way forward. In Jesus' name, Amen.

Faith in Action - Reflect & Recharge on Strengthening Faith

Take a few moments today to write down key insights or lessons you've learned about faith this week. Reflect on how these insights have strengthened your relationship with God.

____

____

____

____

____

This Week's Goals

Specific — What am I led to accomplish and why?

Measurable — How will I know when I have accomplished it?

Achievable — How can I accomplish this goal?

Relevant — Is this the right time for me to be working towards this goal?

Timebound — When do I want to accomplish this goal by?

☑ *Goal 1*

____

____

____

____

☑ *Goal 2*

____

____

____

____

☑ *Goal 3*

____

____

____

____

WEEK 4

Building Healthy Relationships

Today I'm grateful for...

____

____

____

____

____

____

____

____

____

____

____

"You can be a courageous parent transforming with strength & dominion."
—Christy Copeland

Love One Another

"A new command I give you: Love one another. As I have loved you, so you must love one another. By this everyone will know that you are my disciples, if you love one another." — **John 13:34-35**

Today, let's reflect on the command to love one another, especially while dealing with painful emotions. John 13:34-35 calls us to love as Jesus loved us, even in the midst of our struggles.

Loving others can be particularly challenging when we are experiencing pain, disappointment, or heartache. Our natural response might be to withdraw or protect ourselves, making it difficult to extend love to those around us. Yet, Jesus commands us to love one another as He has loved us—unconditionally and sacrificially.

Consider the depth of Jesus' love, shown through His actions and sacrifice. Even in His moments of greatest pain, He chose to love and serve others. This is the love He calls us to emulate. When we love others in the midst of our pain, we demonstrate the transformative power of Christ's love and reveal our identity as His disciples.

Reflect on a time when you found it difficult to love due to your own painful emotions. How did you respond? How might focusing on Jesus' example help you to love more deeply and genuinely, even when it's hard?

Prayer

Heavenly Father, thank You for Your perfect love and the example of Jesus, who loved unconditionally even in the face of suffering. Help us to follow His command to love one another, especially when we are dealing with painful emotions. Fill our hearts with Your love so that we can extend it to others, showing the world that we are Your disciples. Give us the strength to love selflessly and sacrificially, trusting that Your love will heal and restore us. In Jesus' name, Amen.

Faith in Action – Love One Another

Today, take a moment to identify someone in your life who could use an extra measure of love and compassion. Reach out to them with a kind word, a helping hand, or a simple act of service. Let your actions be a reflection of Jesus' love, even if you are overcoming your own painful emotions.

____

____

____

____

____

DAY 23

Effective Communication

"My dear brothers and sisters, take note of this: Everyone should be quick to listen, slow to speak and slow to become angry." — **James 1:19**

As a busy divorced parent, effective communication can often feel like a luxury rather than a necessity. Yet, James 1:19 offers us vital advice: be quick to listen, slow to speak, and slow to become angry. In the midst of our hectic schedules and emotional upheavals, practicing active listening can transform our relationships with our children and others.

Active listening involves giving our full attention to the speaker, understanding their message, and responding with empathy and thoughtfulness. This might seem challenging when you're juggling work, household responsibilities, and parenting, but it's crucial for building trust and understanding.

Reflect on your current communication habits. Do you find yourself rushing conversations or becoming easily frustrated? How often do you truly listen to your children, understanding their feelings and needs? By embracing active listening, you can create a more supportive and harmonious environment at home.

Prayer

Heavenly Father, thank You for the wisdom of Your Word that guides us in our daily lives. Help us as parent leaders to be quick to listen, slow to speak, and slow to become angry, as James 1:19 teaches. Grant us the patience and empathy to truly hear and understand our children and others we interact with. May our communication reflect Your love and grace, bringing peace and unity to our households. In Jesus' name, Amen.

Faith in Action - Effective Communication

Today, make a commitment to practice active listening with your children and those around you. Even in the midst of a busy schedule, take a moment to pause, set aside distractions, and give your full attention to the person speaking. Listen not only to their words but also to their emotions and intentions.

____

____

____

____

____

DAY 24

Boundaries in Relationships

"Above all else, guard your heart, for everything you do flows from it."
— **Proverbs 4:23**

Boundaries are essential for protecting our hearts, especially when rebuilding life and relationships after difficult seasons. Proverbs 4:23 emphasizes the importance of guarding our hearts, not as a way to shut others out, but to ensure we stay grounded in what God has for us. Healthy boundaries allow us to connect with others from a place of strength and clarity, without compromising our well-being or values.

Boundaries are not walls; they're like gates that allow us to choose what enters and what stays out. They help us say "yes" and "no" with wisdom and peace, letting in the things that build us up while keeping out the things that cause harm. In relationships, these boundaries reflect our understanding of our worth and the importance of nurturing what God has entrusted to us, including our mental and emotional health.

Sometimes, setting boundaries may feel uncomfortable, especially with loved ones, but boundaries are a form of love, both for ourselves and for others. By establishing clear expectations, we communicate respect and create space for relationships to flourish in healthy, God-honoring ways. Boundaries empower us to give and receive love more freely, as we're not burdened by resentment or overcommitment.

Take a moment to reflect on your relationships and areas where boundaries may be needed. Are there situations or relationships that drain you or compromise your peace? Ask God for guidance as you set these boundaries, trusting that He is equipping you to steward your relationships well, while keeping Him as the primary guard over your heart.

Prayer

Lord, thank You for the wisdom You provide in Your Word, guiding me to guard my heart with care and purpose. Help me to establish boundaries that protect my heart and honor You. Give me courage to set and communicate these boundaries with love, knowing that they are for my good and the good of those around me. Strengthen me to keep You at the center of all my relationships, and may Your peace guard my heart always.

Faith in Action - Boundaries in Relationships

Identify one area in a relationship where you feel the need for healthier boundaries. Take time today to reflect on how you can communicate this boundary with love and respect. Write down what you'll say or the steps you'll take, and pray for the strength and wisdom to follow through, trusting that God is with you in this process.

____

____

____

____

Forging Strong Family Bonds

"Bear with each other and forgive one another if any of you has a grievance against someone. Forgive as the Lord forgave you. And over all these virtues put on love, which binds them all together in perfect unity."
— Colossians 3:13-14

Today, let's reflect on the importance of forging strong family bonds and leading through values as we rebuild our households. Colossians 3:13-14 provides us with essential guidance on how forgiveness and love can create unity and strength within our families.

Rebuilding a household, especially after a significant life change, requires us to be intentional about forming strong family bonds and leading through core values. Colossians 3:13-14 teaches us to bear with one another, forgive as the Lord forgave us, and to put on love, which binds everything together in perfect unity.

Strong family bonds are founded on the principles of forgiveness and love. When we choose to forgive and show grace to our family members, we build an environment of trust and mutual respect. Love, as the central virtue, brings us together and strengthens our relationships, enabling us to face challenges united.

Reflect on the current state of your family relationships. Are there unresolved conflicts or areas where forgiveness is needed? How can you lead your family by exemplifying love and grace in your daily interactions? By focusing on these virtues, you can rebuild your household with stronger bonds and meaningful values.

Prayer

Heavenly Father, thank You for the wisdom and guidance found in Your Word. Help us to bear with one another and forgive as You have forgiven us. Fill our hearts with Your love, which binds us together in perfect unity. As we rebuild our households, grant us the strength and grace to forge strong family bonds and lead through values rooted in Your truth. In Jesus' name, Amen.

Faith in Action - Forging Strong Family Bonds

Today, take a proactive step towards strengthening your family bonds by addressing any unresolved conflicts. Seek forgiveness where needed and extend grace to your family members. Remember that forgiveness is a journey and begins with a willing heart.

Conflict Resolution

*"Moreover if your brother sins against you, go and tell him his fault
between you and him alone. If he hears you, you have gained your brother.
But if he will not hear, take with you one or two more, that 'by the mouth of
two or three witnesses every word may be established.' And if he refuses to
hear them, tell it to the church. But if he refuses even to hear the church, let
him be to you like a heathen and a tax collector."*
— Matthew 18:15-17

Conflict is inevitable, especially when we are healing from trauma or overcoming the complexities of family relationships. But the way we handle conflict can either tear us apart or bring us closer together.

This passage encourages us to address conflicts directly and privately at first, aiming for reconciliation. If resolution isn't reached, seeking the help of others within our faith community can provide additional support and accountability. Ultimately, the goal is not to win an argument but to restore relationships and foster understanding.

Reflect on a recent disagreement or conflict you experienced within your home. What were the main issues, and how did you initially respond? Take a moment to examine your emotions and reactions.

Now, consider how you could handle the situation differently.

Prayer

Heavenly Father, we come before You today seeking wisdom and guidance in our conflicts. Help us to approach each other with humility and love, just as You have taught us. Give us the courage to speak truth with kindness and the grace to listen with open hearts. May Your Holy Spirit guide our conversations, bringing clarity and healing to our relationships. Lord, teach us to forgive as You have forgiven us, and help us to build homes filled with Your peace and love. In Jesus' name, we pray. Amen.

Faith in Action - Conflict Resolution

How can healthy conflict resolution bring you closer to the vision of the peaceful, God-centered home you're rebuilding? What steps can you take to ensure future conflicts are resolved with grace, understanding, and respect?

____

____

____

____

D A Y   2 7

Encouraging Each Other

*"Therefore encourage one another and
build each other up, just as in fact you are doing."*
— Thessalonians 5:11

In the aftermath of trauma or difficult transitions, the journey to restoration can feel overwhelming. But we are not meant to walk this path alone. The Apostle Paul reminds us of the vital role encouragement plays in our lives. When we uplift one another, we infuse our homes with hope and strength.

Encouragement is not just about kind words; it's about recognizing each other's efforts, celebrating progress, and providing support during challenging times. As we rebuild our homes, let's make a conscious effort to encourage one another daily, fostering an environment where everyone feels valued and motivated.

By consistently practicing encouragement, we can transform our homes into sanctuaries of support and love. Let's commit to building each other up, just as Paul encourages us in 1 Thessalonians 5:11. Together, we can create a nurturing environment where everyone can thrive

- ☐ How can I offer encouragement to my children as we rebuild our home together?
- ☐ Are there any areas in my own heart where I need encouragement?
- ☐ How can I seek support from God and others?

Prayer

Heavenly Father, we come before You with grateful hearts for the gift of community and the power of encouragement. Help us to be sources of light and hope for one another as we rebuild our homes. Teach us to see the best in each other and to speak words that uplift and inspire. May our actions reflect Your love and bring healing to our relationships. Lord, fill our hearts with patience, compassion, and understanding, so that we may build each other up according to Your will. In Jesus' name, we pray. Amen

Faith in Action - Encouraging Each Other

As we walk through the rebuilding process after divorce, it's important to support and uplift each other. Reflect on the ways you can be a source of encouragement for those walking this journey alongside you. Whether it's your children, a co-parent, or even yourself, think about the words and actions that will strengthen and bring hope during this time.

____

____

____

____

____

DAY 28

Reflect and Recharge: Building Healthy Relationships

"Be devoted to one another in love. Honor one another above yourselves."
— Romans 12:10

Reflect & Recharge

As we journey through the process of rebuilding our households, it's essential to focus on cultivating healthy relationships. These relationships form the foundation of a loving, supportive home environment. Today, let's reflect on our progress and insights from the past week, and find comfort in prayer as we rest and meditate on what we've learned.

Take a moment to look back on the past week. What steps have you taken to nurture your relationships? Have you noticed any positive changes in your interactions with family members?

Prayer

Dear Heavenly Father,

Thank You for the gift of family and the opportunity to rebuild our household on the foundation of Your love. As we reflect on the past week, we ask for Your wisdom and guidance to nurture healthy relationships within our home.

Help us to communicate with kindness and honesty, to support each other with love and patience, and to cherish the quality time we spend together. Grant us the grace to forgive and the strength to let go of past hurts.

May our home be a place of peace, joy, and mutual respect. We trust in Your guidance as we continue to build a loving and supportive environment for our family.

In Jesus' name, we pray. Amen.

Faith in Action - Building Healthy Relationships

Take time today to rest and meditate on the learnings from this week. Plan one specific action you can take in the coming week to further strengthen your family relationships. Whether it's scheduling regular family time, practicing active listening, or simply expressing your appreciation for your loved ones, every small step counts.

____

____

____

____

This Week's Goals

Specific — What am I led to accomplish and why?

Measurable — How will I know when I have accomplished it?

Achievable — How can I accomplish this goal?

Relevant — Is this the right time for me to be working towards this goal?

Timebound — When do I want to accomplish this goal by?

☑ *Goal 1*

____

____

____

____

☑ *Goal 2*

____

____

____

____

☑ *Goal 3*

____

____

____

____

WEEK 5

Parenting with Grace

____

____

____

____

____

____

____

____

____

____

____

"You can be a courageous parent transforming with strength & dominion."
—Christy Copeland

Godly Parenting

"Train up a child in the way he should go, and when he is old he will not depart from it." — **Proverbs 22:6**

As parents, we are entrusted with the sacred responsibility of raising our children in the way of the Lord, nurturing their unique gifts, and guiding them toward a future that aligns with God's purpose for their lives. Proverbs 22:6 serves as a powerful reminder that when we intentionally train our children in God's ways, those seeds of faith and wisdom will remain with them throughout their lives.

Raising children is not just about meeting their physical needs or ensuring their academic success. It's about discerning the gifts God has placed within them and fostering an environment where those gifts can flourish. Each child is uniquely crafted by God with talents and abilities meant to glorify Him. As parents, our role is to guide them, pray for them, and trust God to reveal the paths He has designed for them.

In my own parenting journey, it was important that I consistently asked God to reveal each of my children's gifts. I prayed for wisdom to place them in environments that would nurture their talents and help them develop those gifts for God's glory. Over time, I watched them blossom into adults who use their God-given abilities in their careers and personal lives. This is the power of godly parenting—partnering with God to raise children who will fulfill their God-given potential.

Prayer

Heavenly Father, I thank You for the precious gift of parenthood. You have entrusted me with the responsibility of raising my children in Your ways, and I ask for

Your wisdom as I guide them toward their purpose. Lord, reveal to me the unique gifts You've placed within each of my children. Help me to discern how best to nurture those gifts and create an environment where they can grow and thrive.

I commit to praying for my children each day, lifting their needs, their futures, and theiro gifts before You. Lord, place them in the right environments where their talents can be developed and where they can grow closer to You. I trust You to lead them on the path You have prepared, and I ask for Your peace and grace as I continue to walk alongside them. In Jesus' name, Amen

Faith in Action – Godly Parenting

Take a moment to reflect on your child's unique abilities and gifts. Consider how you can create opportunities that nurture those talents. Whether it's enrolling them in a new activity, encouraging them to pursue a passion, or providing a supportive environment at home, identify one action you can take this week to help your child grow in their gifts.

____

____

____

____

Leading by Example

*"For we are His workmanship, created in Christ Jesus for good works, which
God prepared beforehand that we should walk in them."*
— **Ephesians 2:10**

Today, let's reflect on a profound question: Are you a victim of other people's misinterpretation of you? It's easy to let others' misconceptions define us, but we must not attempt to live out these false perceptions and then transfer them to our children.

Being misunderstood by others can be deeply painful. It can cause us to doubt our worth and question our purpose. However, living under the weight of these misinterpretations is not what God intended for us. Ephesians 2:10 reminds us that we are God's masterpiece, created anew in Christ Jesus to fulfill His plans.

When we allow others' misconceptions to shape our identity, we risk passing on these distorted views to our children. Instead, we need to embrace the truth of who we are in Christ and lead our families towards wholeness. There's a better way to live and a better way to guide our children.

God has equipped us with the tools to lead our families to wholeness. By learning and applying the 11 Keys, we can break free from the chains of misinterpretation and step into the fullness of God's purpose for our lives.

Learn about the 11 Keys to leading your family to wholeness and commit to applying them in your daily life. Remember, you are the one God chose to lead your family. Embrace this calling with confidence, knowing that He has equipped you for this purpose.

Prayer

Heavenly Father, thank You for creating us as Your masterpieces. Help us to see ourselves through Your eyes and not through the misinterpretations of others. Give us the strength to reject false identities and to embrace the truth of who we are in Christ. Guide us as we lead our families to wholeness, ensuring that we pass on a legacy of love, faith, and truth to our children. In Jesus' name, Amen.

Faith in Action - Leading by Example

Reflect on the areas of your life where you may have allowed others' misinterpretations to influence your self-view. Write down these false perceptions and then counter them with God's truth from Scripture.

____

____

____

____

____

Patience in Parenting

"But the fruit of the Spirit is love, joy, peace, forbearance, kindness, goodness, faithfulness, gentleness, and self-control."
— Galatians 5:22

Rebuilding a household takes patience, especially in the realm of godly parenting. Galatians 5:22 reminds us that patience, or forbearance, is a fruit of the Spirit—a quality that grows in us as we draw closer to God. Reflect on the challenges you face in your household. Are there moments when impatience gets the best of you?

Consider how embracing the fruits of the Spirit can transform your approach to parenting and bring peace and harmony to your home. Patience isn't just about waiting; it's about maintaining a calm and loving demeanor even in trying times.

Replace with Your Inspiration Well

☐ Practice Mindful Patience: When you feel impatience rising, take a moment to breathe and pray. Ask God to calm your heart and grant you the patience you need in that moment.

☐ Create a Calm Environment: Foster a home environment where peace and calmness are prioritized. This might include setting routines, reducing clutter, or creating quiet spaces for reflection and prayer.

☐ Encourage Open Communication: Allow your children to express their feelings and frustrations without fear of immediate correction or anger. Listen to them with empathy and understanding, showing patience in your responses.

Prayer

Heavenly Father, thank You for the gift of patience. As I work to rebuild my household, fill me with Your Spirit so that love, joy, peace, and patience overflow in my heart. Help me to be patient with my children and myself, understanding that growth and healing take time. Guide me to be a reflection of Your grace in all I do. Amen.

Faith in Action – Patience in Parenting

Think about a recent moment where your patience was tested as a parent. How did you respond, and what might you have done differently to reflect God's patience? What practical steps can you take to cultivate more patience in your parenting?

____

____

____

____

____

Teaching Forgiveness

"For if you forgive other people when they sin against you, your heavenly Father will also forgive you. But if you do not forgive others their sins, your Father will not forgive your sins."
— Matthew 6:14-15

Forgiveness is a cornerstone of rebuilding any household. Matthew 6:14-15 emphasizes the importance of forgiving others as we seek forgiveness from God. In the context of parenting, forgiveness can heal wounds, mend relationships, and foster a loving environment. Reflect on any unresolved conflicts or hurts within your family. Are there areas where forgiveness is needed? Remember, forgiveness doesn't mean forgetting or excusing wrong behavior; it means releasing the burden of resentment and allowing God's grace to work in your heart and home.

Replace with Your Inspiration Well

☐ Initiate Forgiveness: If there are unresolved issues in your household, take the first step toward reconciliation. Approach your family members with humility and a sincere desire to mend relationships.

☐ Teach Forgiveness: Discuss the importance of forgiveness with your children. Share stories from the Bible and personal experiences that highlight the healing power of forgiveness.

☐ Model Forgiveness: Demonstrate forgiveness in your daily.

Prayer

Heavenly Father, thank You for the gift of forgiveness. Help me to forgive those who have hurt me, especially within my family. Teach me to let go of resentment and embrace Your grace. Guide me to be an example of Your love and forgiveness for my children, so they too may learn the power of forgiveness in their lives. Amen.

Faith in Action – Teaching Forgiveness

Today, model forgiveness by letting go of a small grievance. Share with your children how God's love helps you release anger or hurt. This simple act will show them the freedom found in a forgiving heart.

____

____

____

____

____

Nurturing Emotional Health

Do not let any unwholesome talk come out of your mouths, but only what is helpful for building others up according to their needs, that it may benefit those who listen." — **Ephesians 4:29**

Nourishing emotional health is crucial for rebuilding a strong and loving household. Ephesians 4:29 reminds us of the power of our words to either build up or tear down. In godly parenting, it's essential to speak life, encouragement, and love into our children's hearts. Reflect on the language and tone you use at home. Are your words uplifting and affirming? Are you creating an environment where everyone feels valued and supported? Consider how you can be more intentional with your communication to foster emotional well-being in your family.

Last night, I asked my son to show me the art he's been creating for his figure drawing class. As I looked at his work, I was amazed by the incredible detail he captured while illustrating live models. It was clear that he's pouring his heart and talent into each piece. He chuckled and said, "Mom, this is what I have to put up with at school." We both laughed, but deep down, I couldn't help but feel immense pride. He often thinks I make too much out of his artistic talent, but as parents, it's part of our calling to see the gifts in our children—even when they can't see it themselves.

Our influence as parents is powerful. Encouraging our children's gifts is not just about praise, but about nurturing their strengths so they can grow into the people God created them to be. So, to my son, and to all our children: keep going. You are seen, you are valued, and your gifts are a blessing that can touch the world.

Prayer

Heavenly Father, thank You for the power of words. Help me to speak only what is helpful for building up my family. Give me the wisdom to choose my words carefully and the grace to speak with love and kindness. Guide me in creating a nurturing environment where emotional health can flourish. Amen.

Faith in Action – Nurturing Emotional Health

Today, I will take a moment to acknowledge and celebrate one of my child's gifts, reminding them of the beauty God has placed within them. May my encouragement uplift and empower them as they continue to grow.

____

____

____

____

____

DAY 34

Spiritual Growth as a Family

*"These commandments that I give you today are to be on your hearts.
Impress them on your children. Talk about them when you sit at home and
when you walk along the road, when you lie down and when you get up."*
— Deuteronomy 6:6-7

Spiritual growth as a family is foundational to rebuilding and strengthening your household. Deuteronomy 6:6-7 emphasizes the importance of keeping God's commandments in our hearts and teaching them to our children in every aspect of daily life. Reflect on how you can integrate spiritual discussions and practices into your family's routine. Consider the ways you can nurture your family's faith journey together, creating a home environment rooted in God's Word and love.

Replace with Your Inspiration Well

☐ Set a Regular Devotion Time: Choose a specific time each day for family devotion, whether it's in the morning, after dinner, or before bed. Consistency is key to making it a meaningful routine.

☐ Use Age-Appropriate Materials: Select devotional materials and Bible readings that are suitable for all family members. Consider using a family devotional book, children's Bible stories, or age-appropriate scripture readings.

☐ Encourage Participation: Involve every family member in the devotion. Let each person take turns reading scripture, sharing their thoughts, or leading a prayer. This fosters a sense of ownership and engagement.

Remember, spiritual growth is a continuous process that flourishes with dedication and a shared commitment to seeking God together.

Prayer

Heavenly Father, thank You for the gift of family. Help us to grow together in faith and spiritual maturity. Guide us in teaching and living out Your commandments daily. May our home be a place where Your love and wisdom are evident in all we do. Bless our efforts to seek You as a family and strengthen our bond through our shared faith. Amen.

Faith in Action - Spiritual Growth as a Family

In what ways has your family grown spiritually together recently? Reflect on shared moments of prayer, worship, or learning God's Word, and consider how you can continue nurturing your family's faith journey.

Reflect and Recharge: Parenting with Grace

But he said to me, 'My grace is sufficient for you, for my power is made perfect in weakness.' Therefore I will boast all the more gladly about my weaknesses, so that Christ's power may rest on me." — **2 Corinthians 12:9**

As we experience the joys and challenges of parenting, it's easy to feel overwhelmed by our imperfections. We often strive for perfection, fearing that our mistakes might leave lasting impacts on our children. But in these moments of self-doubt, we must remember that God's grace is more than sufficient to cover our shortcomings.

Reflect & Recharge

Take a moment to reflect on the past week. Where have you felt inadequate as a parent? Acknowledge these feelings without judgment. Recognize that your imperfections are not failures, but opportunities for God's grace to shine through. Embrace your weaknesses as spaces where God's strength can manifest.

This week, I invite you to practice parenting with grace. When you encounter a difficult moment with your child, pause and remind yourself of God's unwavering love and grace. Respond with kindness and patience, both towards your child and yourself. At Leaders Wellness Suite, we believe that parenting with grace can transform not only our children's lives but also our own.

Prayer

Heavenly Father, thank You for Your boundless grace that covers all our imperfections. Help us to parent with that same grace, showing our children Your love through our actions and words. Give us the strength to embrace our weaknesses and the wisdom to rely on Your strength. Amen.

Faith in Action – Reflect & Recharge: Parenting with Grace

What specific changes or actions will you implement to create a more grace-filled parenting journey? Write down your thoughts and commit to one action step this week.

____

____

____

____

____

This Week's Goals

Specific — What am I led to accomplish and why?

Measurable — How will I know when I have accomplished it?

Achievable — How can I accomplish this goal?

Relevant — Is this the right time for me to be working towards this goal?

Timebound — When do I want to accomplish this goal by?

☑ *Goal 1*

____

____

____

____

☑ *Goal 2*

____

____

____

☑ *Goal 3*

____

____

____

____

WEEK 6

Embracing
Wellness & Self Care

____

____

____

____

____

____

____

____

____

____

____

"You can be a courageous parent transforming with strength & dominion."
—Christy Copeland

The Importance of Rest

Come to me, all you who are weary and burdened, and I will give you rest."
— Matthew 11:28

In our fast-paced world, rest often feels like a luxury rather than a necessity. We juggle numerous responsibilities, constantly pushing ourselves to the limit. Yet, Jesus invites us to come to Him when we are weary and burdened, promising us rest. This invitation is not just for physical rest but for a deep, soul-refreshing rest that only God can provide.

Embracing God's rest means trusting Him with our burdens and acknowledging that we are not meant to carry them alone. It's about finding peace in His presence and allowing His grace to rejuvenate our spirits. Take a moment to reflect on your life. Are there areas where you feel overwhelmed? Bring these to God, and accept His offer of rest.

The Importance of Sleep: Alongside spiritual rest, sleep is a crucial aspect of our overall restoration. Quality sleep allows our bodies and minds to heal and renew. It affects our mood, our ability to think clearly, and our overall health. Without sufficient sleep, we are more susceptible to stress, anxiety, and a host of physical ailments. Embracing God's rest includes recognizing the need for proper sleep as part of His design for our well-being

Sleep is essential, and when we don't get enough of it, it can be hard to show up as the loving, patient parents we want to be. In fact, sleep-deprived parents often struggle to convey warmth and may react impulsively when they feel frustrated with their children. We've all had those moments, haven't we? But the lack of sleep can affect more than just our patience—it's also closely tied to emotional instability, mental illness, and even depression.

For mothers, specifically, studies have shown that less sleep is connected to fewer positive parenting behaviors, even when other stressors are accounted for. Mothers who struggle to fall asleep also tend to report more dysfunctional parenting practices, which shows just how crucial sleep is for our well-being and for the way we show up for our families.

Prayer

Heavenly Father, thank You for the gift of rest. Help us to trust You with our burdens and to embrace the rest You offer. Teach us to prioritize rest in our lives, understanding that it is essential for our well-being.

Faith in Action - The Importance of Rest

Identify and address any bad habits that may be hindering your ability to rest. Pray for the strength to forgive those who have wronged you, releasing any burdens of resentment and allowing God's peace to fill your heart.

____

____

____

____

DAY 37

Physical and Spiritual Health

Do you not know that your bodies are temples of the Holy Spirit, who is in you, whom you have received from God? You are not your own; you were bought at a price. Therefore honor God with your bodies."
— 1 Corinthians 6:19-20

As we take dominion in our roles as leaders in our households, it's essential to recognize the profound connection between physical health and spiritual health. Our bodies are temples of the Holy Spirit, and we are called to honor God with our physical being. This involves taking care of our health through proper nutrition, exercise, rest, and overall wellness.

Honoring God with our bodies means seeing our physical health as an act of worship. When we prioritize our health, we are better equipped to serve our families, lead effectively, and fulfill the purpose God has for our lives. At Leaders Wellness Suite, we believe that honoring God with our bodies is a vital part of our spiritual and personal well-being.

Guarding Against the Temptation of Addiction: One critical aspect of honoring our bodies is guarding against addictions that can harm our health and spiritual well-being. Addictions can take many forms—substance abuse, excessive screen time, unhealthy eating habits, or other destructive behaviors. These temptations can lead us away from God's path and hinder our ability to lead our households effectively. It's crucial to be vigilant and proactive in addressing any tendencies toward addictive behaviors, seeking God's strength and support in overcoming them.

Prayer

Heavenly Father, thank You for the gift of our bodies and the reminder that they are temples of the Holy Spirit. Help us to honor You by taking care of our physical health. Give us the strength and wisdom to make choices that reflect our commitment to You. Help us guard against the temptations of addiction, seeking Your guidance and support in maintaining healthy, balanced lives.

Faith in Action - Physical and Spiritual Health

Reflect on how you have been treating your body. Are there areas where you could improve? Consider how making healthier choices can enhance not only your well-being but also your spiritual life.

Mental Health Matters

"Finally, brothers and sisters, whatever is true, whatever is noble, whatever is right, whatever is pure, whatever is lovely, whatever is admirable—if anything is excellent or praiseworthy—think about such things."
— Philippians 4:8

Our minds are powerful and profoundly impact how we experience life. Philippians 4:8 encourages us to focus on what is true, noble, right, pure, lovely, admirable, excellent, and praiseworthy. Guarding our minds means intentionally choosing thoughts that uplift and edify us, steering clear of those that lead to anxiety and despair. This practice is essential for maintaining good mental health. At Leaders Wellness Suite, we believe that taking care of our mental health is crucial for our overall well-being and spiritual growth.

Reflect on your thought patterns. Are they aligned with the virtues mentioned in Philippians 4:8? If not, consider how you can redirect your focus towards more positive and life-giving thoughts. Guarding your mind is about being mindful of what you consume—whether it's the media you watch, the conversations you engage in, or the internal dialogue you entertain. It's about creating a mental environment where peace and positivity can flourish.

Creating a safe emotional space for yourself and your children is essential for mental well-being. When we manage our own mental health and stressors effectively, we model resilience and stability for our children. A supportive and nurturing environment helps them feel secure, which encourages them to express their feelings openly and move forward with confidence. It allows them to overcome their own challenges with greater ease, knowing they have a loving and understanding support system.

Today, take time to identify the stressors in your life. These could be certain relationships, work pressures, financial concerns, or even personal expectations. Write them down and bring them before God in prayer. Ask for His guidance in addressing each stressor, whether it means making practical changes, seeking support, or simply trusting Him more deeply.

Prayer

Heavenly Father, thank You for the wisdom in Your Word that guides us in maintaining a healthy mind. Help us to guard our minds and focus on what is true and uplifting. Give us the discernment to recognize and address any negative thought patterns.

Faith in Action – Mental Health Matters

What are some specific stressors or negative thought patterns that may be affecting my mental health or the emotional well-being of my children, and how can I address them to create a safer, more supportive environment?

____

____

____

____

DAY 39

Nutrition and Well Being

"And God said, 'See, I have given you every herb that yields seed which is on the face of all the earth, and every tree whose fruit yields seed; to you it shall be for food.' — **Genesis 1:29**

As we rebuild our lives and prepare to establish a lasting legacy for our families, it's important to recognize that the health of our bodies is not only a blessing but a responsibility. God, in His infinite wisdom, provided us with the nourishment we need through His creation. Genesis 1:29 is a reminder that from the very beginning, God cared about our well-being, providing us with fruits, vegetables, and grains to sustain and nurture our bodies.

I've become more aware of the crucial role nutrition plays in our overall health—physically, mentally, and spiritually. As we take steps to rebuild our households, we are also preparing a foundation for future generations. A key part of this preparation is caring for the bodies God has given us, not just for our sake, but for the sake of those we love.

By choosing to nourish ourselves with wholesome, healthy foods, we honor the bodies God has entrusted to us and set an example for our families. This awareness calls us to be more intentional about what we consume and how it affects our energy, mood, and ability to serve God and others. It's not just about physical health; it's about being equipped to fulfill God's purpose for our lives.

As you reflect on your health journey, consider how you can take greater responsibility for your nutrition, knowing that it is a vital part of your overall well-being. By making small, intentional changes, you are not only caring for yourself but also setting a precedent for your children and family, teaching them the importance of stewarding their health as a gift from God.

Prayer

Heavenly Father, thank You for providing all that we need for our health and well-being. I am grateful for the nourishment You have created through the fruits of the earth. Lord, help me to take responsibility for my health, making wise choices that honor the body You have given me. Guide me as I plan meals and make decisions that will sustain me physically, mentally, and spiritually.

As I rebuild my household and prepare for my family's legacy, I pray for strength, discipline, and wisdom to prioritize nutrition and well-being. Help me to be a model of health for my family, teaching them to care for their bodies as an act of worship and stewardship. Thank You, Lord, for the opportunity to grow in this area of my life. In Jesus' name, Amen.

Faith in Action – Nutrition and Well Being

This week, take time to plan healthy meals for yourself and your family. Start by incorporating more fruits, vegetables, and whole grains into your diet, and seek to eliminate processed foods where possible. Consider meal prepping or setting aside time to research nutritious recipes that can become part of your household's routine.

DAY 40

Exercise as Worship

"For physical training is of some value, but godliness has value for all things, holding promise for both the present life and the life to come."
— 1 Timothy 4:8

Often, we think of worship as singing, praying, or attending church. However, worship encompasses every aspect of our lives, including how we care for our bodies. In 1 Timothy 4:8, Paul acknowledges the value of physical training, emphasizing that it holds benefits for our earthly life. By taking care of our physical health, we honor the body God has given us, which is a temple of the Holy Spirit (1 Corinthians 6:19-20).

Seeing physical activity as a form of worship changes our perspective on exercise. It's not just about achieving fitness goals or aesthetics; it's about stewarding our bodies as an act of gratitude and obedience to God. When we engage in physical activity, we can do so with a heart of worship, offering our efforts to God and seeking to honor Him with our health and well-being.

Here are some practical steps to integrate exercise into your life:

☐ Set Expectation: Begin each exercise session with a prayer, dedicating your efforts to God and asking for strength and endurance.

☐ Find Joy in Movement: Choose activities that you enjoy and that make you feel connected to God's creation, like hiking, dancing, or swimming.

☐ Be Consistent: Aim to include physical activity in your routine regularly. This consistency not only benefits your physical health but also your spiritual discipline.

☐ Listen to Your Body: Pay attention to your body's needs and limits. Rest when necessary and avoid pushing yourself to the point of harm.

Prayer

Heavenly Father, thank You for the gift of our bodies and the ability to move and be active. Help us to see exercise not just as a task but as an opportunity to worship You. Guide us in taking care of our bodies in a way that honors You and reflects Your love.

As we move forward, let's commit to incorporating exercise into our daily routines as an act of worship. May our exercise routines be a reflection of our love for You and our desire to honor You with our whole selves. Amen.

Faith in Action - Exercise as Worship

Reflect on your current daily routine. How can you intentionally incorporate more movement into your day? Whether it's taking a walk, stretching, or doing a short workout, write down a few simple ways you can increase your physical activity this week. How does viewing movement as a gift from God change your perspective on exercise?

____

____

____

____

____

Embracing Happiness Despite Disapproval

The joy of the Lord is your strength."
— Nehemiah 8:10

Have you ever noticed that your happiness can sometimes be met with disapproval or even disappointment by others? It can be disheartening when those around us, perhaps even those we considered friends, seem to be waiting for us to fail. But as followers of Christ, our joy is not dependent on the approval of others. The joy of the Lord is our strength, and it is this divine joy that sustains us through both triumphs and trials.

It's crucial to remember that everyone's journey is different. Some people might struggle with their own issues of envy or insecurity, causing them to react negatively to your happiness. While it's natural to seek approval and validation, we must anchor our sense of worth and joy in God's love and promises, rather than in the fleeting opinions of others.

It's okay to not have everyone's approval. In fact, it's more than okay—it's liberating. When we stop seeking validation from those who do not genuinely support us, we can focus on what truly matters: our relationship with God, our personal growth, and the joy that comes from living authentically. By embracing this mindset, we allow ourselves to flourish and shine, regardless of the negativity that may surround us. At Leaders Wellness Suite, we believe in embracing our happiness and standing strong, even when others may not support our joy and success.

Prayer

Heavenly Father, thank You for the joy that You provide, a joy that is steadfast and true. Help us to find our strength in You and to embrace our happiness, even when it disappoints those who were waiting for us to fail. Give us the courage to live authentically and to seek approval only from You. Lord, guide us in finding peace and confidence in Your approval. Help us to let go of the need for validation from those who do not support us and to embrace the joy that You provide. May we stand firm in our happiness, knowing that it is a testament to Your goodness and grace. Amen.

Faith in Action – Embracing Happiness Despite Disapproval

Today, reflect on areas where you might be seeking approval from others and how this impacts your happiness. Take steps to shift your focus towards God's affirmation and the joy that comes from His presence. Celebrate your successes, no matter how big or small, and remember that your worth is not defined by the opinions of others but by the love of God.

DAY 42

Spiritual Refreshing

"He restores my soul; He leads me in the paths of righteousness for His name's sake." — **Psalm 23:3 (NKJV)**

Life's demands can often leave us feeling drained, overwhelmed, and distant from the peace that God offers. Just as our bodies need physical rest and nourishment, our souls require regular spiritual care to remain strong and resilient. Psalm 23:3 reminds us that God is our shepherd, restoring our souls and guiding us along paths of righteousness.

Spiritual self-care involves intentionally creating space to connect with God and allow Him to refresh your spirit. Whether through prayer, meditation on scripture, worship, or simply resting in His presence, these practices help to realign our hearts and minds with God's will. In these moments, we find renewal, strength, and the peace that surpasses all understanding.

As you reflect on your spiritual self-care, consider the ways in which you can invite God into your daily routine. Make space for His presence, and trust that He will lead you to still waters where your soul can be refreshed.

Prayer

Heavenly Father, thank You for being the restorer of our souls. I ask for Your guidance in prioritizing spiritual self-care in my life. Help me to set aside dedicated time to spend with You, to be renewed and refreshed by Your presence. Lead me in the paths of righteousness, and grant me the wisdom to recognize when I need to pause and reconnect with You. May my soul find peace and restoration in You alone. In Jesus' name, I pray, Amen.

Faith in Action - Spiritual Refreshing

This week, carve out intentional time each day for spiritual renewal. Whether it's a few minutes in the morning, a moment of quiet reflection during the day, or a time of worship in the evening, commit to refreshing your soul through regular spiritual practices. Let this be your pathway to peace and strength in the Lord.

____

____

____

____

____

Emotional Well-being

"A cheerful heart is good medicine, but a crushed spirit dries up the bones."
— **Proverbs 17:22**

As we move through the journey of rebuilding our household, it's essential to prioritize our emotional well-being. Proverbs 17:22 reminds us that a cheerful heart is like good medicine. Joy and laughter have the power to heal, uplift, and strengthen us during challenging times.

In the midst of the responsibilities and tasks that come with rebuilding, we must remember to create moments of joy. Laughter can lighten our burdens, help us connect more deeply with one another, and bring a sense of peace to our hearts. It's through these moments of joy that our spirits are renewed, and our homes are filled with warmth and love.

Embracing joy doesn't mean ignoring our challenges—it means choosing to find light even in the darkest times. Whether it's sharing a funny story, playing a game, or simply taking time to enjoy each other's company, these small moments can have a profound impact on our emotional health and the atmosphere of our home.

As we continue to rebuild, let's remember that joy is not just a fleeting emotion—it's a powerful force that can renew our spirits and bring healing to our hearts. May your home be filled with laughter, love, and the joy that only God can provide.

Prayer

Dear Heavenly Father, thank You for the gift of joy and laughter. As we rebuild our household, help us to find moments of joy in our daily lives. Remind us to take time for activities that bring us closer together and lift our spirits. Guide us to create a home where joy is abundant and laughter is a common sound. Amen.

Faith in Action – Emotional Well Being

This week, make it a priority to engage in at least one activity that brings joy to your household. Whether it's a family game night, watching a funny movie together, or taking a walk in nature, intentionally create a space for laughter and happiness in your home. Watch how these moments can transform your emotional well-being and strengthen your family bonds.

____

____

____

____

____

DAY 44

Taking Care of Ourselves Isn't Selfish

"Then, because so many people were coming and going that they did not even have a chance to eat, he said to them, 'Come with me by yourselves to a quiet place and get some rest.'" — **Mark 6:31**

As we focus on rebuilding our household, it's easy to become consumed with tasks, responsibilities, and the needs of others. However, Jesus himself reminds us in Mark 6:31 of the importance of stepping away from the busyness to rest and recharge. Taking care of yourself isn't selfish; it's a necessary practice that allows us to serve others more effectively.

When we neglect our own well-being, we risk burnout, frustration, and a diminished capacity to care for those around us. True care for oneself is about honoring the body, mind, and spirit that God has given us. It's about understanding that we can't pour from an empty cup—taking time for ourselves is an essential part of being able to give to our family and loved ones.

Let's remember that taking care of yourself is not about indulgence but about sustenance. It's taking the time to nourish our souls so that we can continue to walk in the purpose God has set before us. By embracing this practice, we acknowledge that we are valuable, and that caring for ourselves is part of being good stewards of the life God has blessed us with.

Prayer

Dear Heavenly Father, thank You for the reminder that taking care of ourselves is a part of Your design for us. Help us to understand the importance of taking time to rest, reflect, and recharge. Teach us to see this practice not as an act of selfishness but as an essential part of maintaining the strength we need to fulfill our roles in our families and communities.

Lord, guide us as we schedule regular moments to take care of ourselves. Whether it's setting aside time for prayer, a peaceful walk, or simply a moment of silence with You, help us to prioritize these moments of rest. May we find refreshment in Your presence and emerge with renewed energy and purpose.

We trust that as we take care of ourselves, You will continue to pour Your grace and strength into our lives, enabling us to rebuild our households with love, patience, and joy. In Jesus' name, we pray. Amen.

Faith in Action - Taking Care of Ourselves Isn't Selfish

Take time this week to intentionally schedule activities that allow you to take care of yourself. Whether it's a quiet morning with a cup of tea, a walk in nature, or a moment of prayer and reflection, remember that caring for yourself is also caring for those you love.

DAY 45

Creating a Support System

Two are better than one, because they have a good return for their labor: If either of them falls down, one can help the other up. But pity anyone who falls and has no one to help them up." — **Ecclesiastes 4:9-10**

In times of rebuilding, whether after a major life change or during challenging seasons, the importance of a strong support system cannot be overstated. Ecclesiastes reminds us that we are not meant to walk this journey alone. When we have others by our side, we not only share the load, but we also experience the comfort of knowing we are supported and uplifted.

Building a network of support is essential as we work to restore our household. This might mean reconnecting with trusted friends, leaning on family members, or even seeking out new relationships within our community. A strong support system provides not just practical help, but emotional and spiritual encouragement as well. Remember, God often uses the people in our lives to extend His love, wisdom, and strength to us.

As parents, we have the unique opportunity to model what a healthy, supportive friendship looks like for our children. By surrounding ourselves with positive influences and nurturing those relationships, we show our children the value of connection, trust, and mutual support. When they see us reaching out and being a good friend to others, they learn how to build their own support networks, which will be invaluable as they grow and face their own challenges.

Prayer

Heavenly Father, thank You for the people You have placed in our lives who support and uplift us. Help us to recognize the importance of community and to reach out to those who can walk alongside us during this time of rebuilding. Give us the courage to ask for help when needed and the wisdom to be a support to others as well. Lord, guide us as we cultivate these relationships and let them be a source of Your grace and love in our lives. Show us how to be an example of a healthy, supportive friend for our children, so they too can build strong, meaningful relationships. In Jesus' name, Amen.

Faith in Action - Creating a Support System

This week, take a step toward strengthening your support system. Reach out to a friend or family member you trust, and share what's on your heart. Also, consider how you can demonstrate being a good friend to your child. Let them see you investing in relationships that uplift and encourage, teaching them the value of community through your actions.

Healthy Boundaries

""But let your 'Yes' be 'Yes,' and your 'No,' 'No.' For whatever is more than these is from the evil one." — **Matthew 5:37**

As we rebuild our households, establishing healthy boundaries is crucial. Boundaries help us protect our emotional, mental, and spiritual well-being while fostering respect and understanding within our families. They enable us to clearly communicate our needs and expectations, ensuring that our relationships are built on mutual respect and trust.

Jesus' teaching in Matthew 5:37 reminds us of the power of simplicity and clarity in our communication. When we are clear about our 'Yes' and 'No,' we honor both ourselves and others. Setting boundaries is not about shutting people out; it's about creating a safe space where love and respect can flourish.

Trauma can significantly affect a person's ability to set and maintain healthy boundaries. Some who have experienced trauma might have difficulty asserting themselves or may be overly accommodating, allowing others to overstep their personal limits. This can lead to further emotional harm and hinder the healing process.

Prayer

Heavenly Father, thank You for the wisdom to understand the importance of boundaries in our lives. Help us to identify the areas where we need to establish personal boundaries, and grant us the courage to enforce them with love and grace.

Today, I commit to identifying the boundaries I need in my life to maintain my well-being and to protect the harmony within my household. Guide me as I take steps to communicate these boundaries clearly and kindly, ensuring that they are respected by those around me.

Lord, may our homes be places of peace and mutual respect, where each 'Yes' and 'No' is honored, and where love and understanding abound. In Jesus' name, Amen.

Faith in Action - Healthy Boundaries

How can I distinguish between emotions that need to be acknowledged and processed, versus emotions that might be best set aside in the moment to make a clearer decision?

____

____

____

____

____

Reflect & Recharge on Embracing Wellness & Self-Care

Beloved, I pray that you may prosper in all things and be in health, just as your soul prospers." — **3 John 1:2**

As we reach the end of this week, it's time to pause and review the insights and progress we've made in embracing wellness and self-care. Throughout the week, we've been reminded that taking care of ourselves—physically, emotionally, and spiritually—is not just beneficial, but essential for living a life that honors God.

Perhaps this week, you've taken steps to nourish your body with healthier choices, dedicated moments to rest, or simply allowed yourself to be still in God's presence. Maybe you've recognized areas where you've been neglecting your well-being, and you're beginning to make changes to restore balance. Whatever your journey has looked like, take a moment now to reflect on the progress you've made, no matter how small.

Wellness is a journey, not a destination. It requires continuous effort, intentionality, and grace. As you review the week's learnings, consider how these insights can be carried forward into your daily life. How can you continue to prioritize your well-being and make self-care a consistent part of your routine? Remember, embracing wellness isn't just about feeling good; it's about being equipped to fulfill the purpose God has placed on your life.

Prayer

Heavenly Father, thank You for the wisdom and insight You've provided this week as we've focused on wellness and self-care. Help us to internalize these lessons and apply them to our daily lives. We acknowledge that our bodies and minds are gifts from You, and we desire to honor You by caring for them well.

As we close out this week, Lord, we ask for the strength to continue prioritizing our health and well-being. Guide us to rest and meditate on the truths we've learned. May we find peace and renewal in Your presence, and may our commitment to self-care reflect our trust in You.

Today, I commit to taking a moment of rest and meditation, allowing the week's insights to settle in my heart. Help me to carry these lessons forward, so that I may live a life that is not just productive, but also filled with Your peace and joy.

In Jesus' name, Amen.

Faith in Action – Reflect & Recharge on Embracing Wellness and Self-Care

Reflect on how far you've come, and trust that with God's guidance, you can continue to grow in your journey towards a healthier, more balanced life. Take time to rest and meditate on these learnings, allowing God to renew your strength and fill you with His peace.

This Week's Goals

Specific — What am I led to accomplish and why?

Measurable — How will I know when I have accomplished it?

Achievable — How can I accomplish this goal?

Relevant — Is this the right time for me to be working towards this goal?

Timebound — When do I want to accomplish this goal by?

☑ *Goal 1*

____

____

____

____

☑ *Goal 2*

____

____

____

____

☑ *Goal 3*

____

____

____

____

WEEK 7

Strengthening Relationships with Other Parents & Extended Family

Today I'm grateful for...

____

____

____

____

____

____

____

____

____

____

____

____

"You can be a courageous parent transforming with strength & dominion."
—Christy Copeland

Co-Parenting with Grace

Bear with each other and forgive one another if any of you has a grievance against someone. Forgive as the Lord forgave you."
— Colossians 3:13

Co-parenting can be one of the most challenging aspects of raising children after a separation or divorce. It requires constant communication, cooperation, and, most importantly, grace. When emotions run high and past wounds resurface, it's easy to let frustration and bitterness take over. But as believers, we're called to lead this journey with a heart full of forgiveness and understanding.

Colossians 3:13 reminds us to bear with one another and forgive as the Lord forgave us. This doesn't mean ignoring the hurt or pretending that challenges don't exist; rather, it means choosing to extend grace in the same way God extends it to us. Co-parenting with grace means making a conscious effort to put the well-being of your children first, even when it's difficult. It's about creating a peaceful environment where your children can thrive, free from the burden of tension between their parents.

As you reflect on your co-parenting journey, consider the ways you can bring more grace into your interactions. Are there unresolved grievances that need to be addressed with forgiveness? How can you approach difficult conversations with a spirit of understanding, seeking peace rather than conflict?

Remember, co-parenting with grace isn't just about getting along for the sake of the children; it's about honoring God in the way you navigate this relationship. By leaning on His strength and following His example of forgiveness, you can create a foundation of peace and stability for your children.

Prayer

Heavenly Father, thank You for the grace and forgiveness You continually offer us. As we handle the complexities of co-parenting, we ask for Your guidance and strength. Help us to reflect Your love in our interactions with our co-parent, choosing to forgive and extend grace even when it's hard.

Lord, we commit to practicing grace in our co-parenting situations. Show us how to approach every conversation with a heart of understanding, seeking what is best for our children and honoring You in all that we do. Help us to forgive past hurts and focus on building a peaceful and cooperative relationship moving forward.

Today, I choose to release any bitterness or resentment I may be holding onto. I ask for Your help in seeing my co-parent through Your eyes, with compassion and understanding. Guide my words and actions so that they reflect Your grace and love.

In Jesus' name, Amen.

Faith in Action - Co-Parenting with Grace

Reflect on specific situations where extending grace could shift the dynamic positively and consider how this approach aligns with God's call to forgive as He has forgiven us.

____

____

____

____

Communicating Effectively with Your Co-Parent

*Do not let any unwholesome talk come out of your mouths, but only what is helpful for building others up according to their needs, that it may benefit those who listen." — **Ephesians 4:29***

Co-parenting can be challenging, especially when skepticism or past hurts cloud the relationship. Yet, as followers of Christ, we are called to a higher standard of communication—one that builds up rather than tears down, even when it's difficult.

Ephesians 4:29 reminds us of the power our words hold. Positive communication isn't just about being polite; it's about speaking life into situations where there may be doubt or distrust. When we choose our words carefully, focusing on what is helpful and constructive, we create an environment where healing and cooperation can flourish. This is especially crucial in co-parenting, where the well-being of our children is at stake.

It's important to acknowledge that skepticism may exist, whether from past experiences or unresolved issues. However, by intentionally communicating with kindness, clarity, and respect, we can begin to break down barriers. Our goal isn't just to convey information but to foster an atmosphere of mutual respect and understanding, which benefits everyone involved—especially our children.

As you reflect on your co-parenting journey, consider how your words and tone can either build up or hinder progress. Are you communicating in a way that aligns with the teachings of Christ? Are your words bringing peace, or are they adding to the tension? Remember, positive communication is a powerful tool that can transform even the most difficult relationships.

Prayer

Heavenly Father, thank You for the wisdom found in Your Word, reminding us of the importance of our communication. Help us to speak with kindness, grace, and wisdom, especially in challenging situations like co-parenting. We ask for Your guidance in choosing our words carefully, so that they may build up and encourage rather than tear down.

Lord, we recognize that effective communication requires effort, patience, and a heart aligned with Your will. Today, we commit to implementing strategies that reflect Your love, such as active listening, speaking with empathy, and addressing conflicts calmly. Help us to overcome skepticism with faith, trusting that You can bring peace and understanding into our co-parenting relationships.

In Jesus' name, Amen.

Faith in Action - Communicating Effectively with Your Co-Parent

Reflect on how Ephesians 4:29 can guide your conversations with your co-parent this week. What steps can you take to embrace positive communication, even in challenging moments? How might this shift in communication impact your relationship and set an example for your children? Write down one specific way you can apply this teaching in your next interaction.

____

____

____

____

Building a United Front

it is possible, as far as it depends on you, live at peace with everyone."
— **Romans 12:18**

Co-parenting can be challenging under the best of circumstances, but when the other parent is willfully uncooperative, it can feel nearly impossible to present a unified front. Yet, as believers, we are called to do everything within our power to live at peace with others, even when they make it difficult. This includes the often frustrating task of co-parenting after a divorce.

In these situations, it's essential to remember that your children's well-being must remain the top priority. While you may not be able to control the actions or attitudes of your co-parent, you can control how you respond. Your approach to co-parenting can still reflect unity and stability, even if the other parent is resistant.

Presenting a unified front doesn't always mean perfect agreement—it means consistent effort to do what is best for your children. It may require more patience, prayer, and wisdom, but God's grace is sufficient to guide you through. By maintaining a calm and focused attitude, you can demonstrate to your children that they are loved and cared for, despite any discord.

Reflect on how you can continue to seek unity in your parenting approach, even in difficult circumstances. This might mean setting firm but respectful boundaries, being the peacemaker, or finding alternative ways to communicate effectively. Trust that God sees your efforts and will honor your commitment to raising your children in a loving and stable environment.

Prayer

Heavenly Father, You know the challenges I face in co-parenting, especially when the other parent is uncooperative. I ask for Your strength and guidance as I seek to build a united front for the sake of my children. Help me to approach every interaction with grace, patience, and wisdom.

Lord, give me the courage to stand firm in my commitment to my children's well-being, even when it's difficult. Help me to find ways to promote peace and cooperation, and when those efforts fall short, remind me that You are in control. Guide my heart to forgive and to trust that You will work all things for good, even in challenging circumstances.

In Jesus' name, Amen.

Faith in Action – Building a United Front

Write about the values and goals you want to prioritize in your parenting, even when facing opposition from your co-parent. Think about the long-term impact of these values on your children, and how you can consistently model them, regardless of your co-parent's cooperation.

____

____

____

____

Forging Strong Bonds with Extended Family

But Ruth replied, 'Don't urge me to leave you or to turn back from you. Where you go I will go, and where you stay I will stay. Your people will be my people and your God my God. Where you die I will die, and there I will be buried. May the Lord deal with me, be it ever so severely, if even death separates you and me.'" — **Ruth 1:16-17**

The story of Ruth and Naomi is a powerful example of the strength and loyalty that can exist within family relationships. Ruth's commitment to her mother-in-law, even after the loss of her husband, is a testament to the deep bonds that can be forged within extended families. In a world where relationships can often become strained or distant, the story of Ruth reminds us of the importance of staying connected to our extended family members.

Extended family relationships can provide us with a sense of belonging, history, and support. These bonds are often a source of wisdom, love, and encouragement, offering a broader community for us and our children. Yet, it's easy to let these relationships fade due to the busyness of life, misunderstandings, or physical distance.

This week, reflect on the relationships you have with your extended family. Are there bonds that need to be strengthened or rekindled? Consider the ways in which these connections can bring richness and stability to your life and the lives of your children. Like Ruth, who chose to stay close to Naomi despite the challenges they faced, we too can choose to invest in our extended family, finding strength and joy in these relationships.

Prayer

Heavenly Father, thank You for the gift of family and the deep bonds that can be formed within it. I'm grateful for the extended family members You've placed in my life and the support and love they can provide. Help me to see the value in these relationships and to prioritize them, even when life gets busy.

Lord, give me the courage to reach out and reconnect with those family members I may have grown distant from. Help me to mend any broken ties and to build strong, lasting bonds that reflect Your love and grace. Guide my heart to be open and willing to invest time and energy into these relationships, knowing that they are a blessing from You.

In Jesus' name, Amen.

Faith in Action - Forging Strong Bonds with Extended Family

Reflect on how reconnecting and expressing love can deepen these relationships. How might this step bring growth and healing to your family? Write down your plan and any feelings that arise as you take this step toward strengthening your family ties.

DAY 52

Managing In-Law Relationships

"Can two walk together, unless they are agreed?"
— **Amos 3:3**

Divorce often complicates relationships with in-laws, creating tension and uncertainty about how to operate this new dynamic. Despite the changes in your marital status, these relationships can still play a significant role in your life and the lives of your children. Amos 3:3 reminds us of the importance of agreement and unity, but what happens when harmony seems elusive?

Living at peace with everyone, including your in-laws, is not always easy, especially when emotions are high and past grievances linger. However, God calls us to be peacemakers and to do our part to live in harmony with those around us. This doesn't mean that you have to agree on everything or ignore your own boundaries, but it does mean striving for respect and understanding in your interactions.

Managing these relationships requires wisdom, patience, and a willingness to extend grace. Whether you are dealing with tension, misunderstandings, or hurtful behavior, seek to approach each situation with a heart of reconciliation. Reflect on how you can contribute to a more peaceful dynamic, even if it means taking the first step toward healing.

It's also important to protect your own well-being and the well-being of your children. Establish clear and healthy boundaries that allow for peaceful interactions without compromising your values or emotional health. Remember, fostering peace doesn't mean tolerating toxic behavior—it means choosing to respond with love and wisdom, even in difficult situations.

Prayer

Heavenly Father, thank You for the relationships You have placed in my life, including those with my in-laws. I acknowledge that these relationships can be challenging, especially after divorce, but I desire to live at peace with everyone as much as it depends on me.

Lord, grant me the wisdom and grace to manage these relationships in a way that honors You. Help me to extend forgiveness where it's needed, to set healthy boundaries, and to approach each interaction with a heart of peace. I ask for Your guidance in resolving conflicts and for the strength to be a peacemaker in my family.

In Jesus' name, Amen.

Faith in Action – Managing In-Law Relationships

Today, I commit to taking a step toward fostering peace with my in-laws. Whether it's through a conversation, an act of kindness, or simply praying for them, I choose to pursue harmony. Write down your plan and any feelings that arise as you take this step toward strengthening your family ties.

____

____

____

____

Grandparents as a Generational Blessing

"Children's children are a crown to the aged, and parents are the pride of their children." — **Proverbs 17:6**

In the process of rebuilding our households after a significant life change, such as divorce, we often focus on immediate needs and adjustments. However, it's essential not to overlook the profound blessing of grandparents. As Proverbs 17:6 beautifully illustrates, grandchildren are a crown to their grandparents, symbolizing the joy and pride that flows through the generations.

Grandparents play a unique and irreplaceable role in the family dynamic. They carry with them a wealth of wisdom, life experience, and love that can be a stabilizing force during times of transition. Their stories and traditions help to root children in a sense of history and belonging, providing continuity even when everything else feels uncertain.

Valuing the role of grandparents in your children's lives means recognizing the richness they add to your family. Whether they're offering guidance, sharing a laugh, or simply being a loving presence, grandparents contribute to the emotional and spiritual well-being of your household. They are a generational blessing, weaving together the past, present, and future in a way that strengthens the entire family.

As you rebuild your household, consider how you can more intentionally involve grandparents in your children's lives. This might mean planning regular visits, encouraging the sharing of family stories, or simply ensuring that your children spend quality time with their grandparents. By honoring and valuing their role, you create opportunities for your children to be richly blessed by the love and wisdom that only grandparents can provide.

Prayer

Heavenly Father, thank You for the gift of grandparents and the unique blessing they bring to our lives. We are grateful for their love, wisdom, and the deep connection they provide across generations. As we work to rebuild our household, help us to remember the invaluable role that grandparents play in the lives of our children.

Lord, guide us to honor and cherish the relationship between our children and their grandparents. Show us how to create meaningful opportunities for them to connect and bond. May the presence of grandparents be a source of comfort, stability, and joy as we navigate this season of rebuilding.

In Jesus' name, Amen.

Faith in Action - Grandparents as a Generational Blessing

Today, I commit to planning a special activity that will allow my children to spend quality time with their grandparents. Whether it's a shared meal, a storytelling session, or a simple walk in the park, I will prioritize these moments to ensure that the generational blessings flow abundantly within our family.

Sibling Relationships

"Finally, all of you, be like-minded, be sympathetic, love one another, be compassionate and humble." — **1 Peter 3:8**

As we work to rebuild our households after a significant life change, such as divorce, one of the most crucial aspects to focus on is fostering strong, healthy sibling relationships. Sibling bonds can either be a source of tremendous support and comfort or a source of ongoing strife and conflict. The Bible encourages us in 1 Peter 3:8 to be like-minded, sympathetic, loving, compassionate, and humble—qualities that are vital for promoting harmony among siblings.

In the midst of family transitions, it's natural for tensions to arise. Children may express their emotions through rivalry, arguments, or withdrawal, and these behaviors can easily lead to discord. However, as parents, we have the unique opportunity to guide our children toward peace and unity. Promoting harmony among siblings doesn't mean eliminating all disagreements, but it does mean teaching them to handle conflicts with love, understanding, and grace.

Encouraging siblings to see each other as allies rather than competitors is key to removing strife. When we emphasize the importance of family unity and the value of each child's role in the family, we help them understand that their relationship with each other is a lifelong blessing. It's also important to model these values by demonstrating love, patience, and forgiveness in our interactions.

As you reflect on the dynamics within your household, consider how you can foster an environment where your children feel safe to express themselves, yet are also encouraged to show empathy and kindness to one another. Building a home where siblings support and uplift each other is not only possible but a beautiful testament to God's love at work in your family.

Prayer

Heavenly Father, thank You for the gift of family and the special bond that siblings share. I pray that You would help me foster an environment of love, peace, and unity in our home. Remove any seeds of strife or discord that may have taken root, and replace them with understanding, compassion, and humility.

Lord, give me the wisdom to guide my children in building strong, supportive relationships with one another. Help me to model the qualities You desire—sympathy, love, and compassion—in my own interactions. I ask that You bless the relationships between my children, helping them to grow closer together and to see each other as lifelong friends and allies.

In Jesus name, Amen

Faith in Action - Sibling Relationships

Today, I commit to encouraging sibling bonding activities that promote unity and understanding. Whether through shared chores, fun outings, or simply spending quality time together, I will seek ways to strengthen the ties that bind my children together. May our home be a place of peace and harmony, reflecting God's love to the world.

____

____

____

____

Extended Family Gatherings

"Behold, how good and how pleasant it is for brethren to dwell together in unity!" — **Psalm 133:1**

Divorce often brings significant changes to family dynamics, leaving many to wonder how to rebuild a sense of unity and connection. While the family structure may have shifted, the bonds that hold you together can still be strong and meaningful. One of the most powerful ways to foster this connection is through extended family gatherings, where new memories can be created and cherished.

Psalm 133:1 beautifully captures the joy that comes from family unity. Even after a divorce, these moments of togetherness can serve as a reminder that you are still part of a loving, supportive network. Extended family gatherings provide an opportunity to celebrate the bonds that remain and to create new, positive memories that can help heal and strengthen your family.

These gatherings can be a source of healing, offering a space where both you and your children can experience the comfort and joy of being surrounded by loved ones. Whether it's a holiday celebration, a birthday party, or simply a weekend barbecue, these moments allow for the sharing of stories, laughter, and love—elements that are crucial as you move forward together.

As you reflect on the importance of family unity, consider how you can bring your loved ones together in a way that fosters connection and joy. These gatherings don't have to be extravagant; what matters most is the intention behind them—building and maintaining the bonds that hold your family together, even as you create new traditions and memories.

Prayer

Heavenly Father, thank You for the gift of family and the joy that comes from being united with loved ones. In times of change and transition, we ask for Your guidance in maintaining and strengthening our family bonds. Help us to see the beauty in our relationships and to cherish the time we have together.

Lord, as we move forward after a divorce, I pray for Your wisdom in organizing gatherings that bring our family closer. May these moments of unity be filled with Your love and peace, creating new memories that will bless us for years to come. Guide me in finding the right opportunities to bring my family together and in fostering an environment where everyone feels welcomed and valued.

In Jesus' name, Amen.

Faith in Action - Extended Family Gatherings

As you think about bringing your extended family together, what steps can you take to make your next gathering meaningful and memorable? Reflect on how you can create an atmosphere of joy, healing, and unity, trusting God to strengthen the bonds within your family.

____

____

____

____

Supporting Each Other's Growth

Therefore encourage one another and build each other up, just as in fact you are doing." — **1 Thessalonians 5:11**

One of the greatest gifts we can offer our family members is unwavering support for their growth and development. In a world that often focuses on individual success, fostering a culture of encouragement within the family is vital. It strengthens bonds, builds confidence, and creates an environment where everyone can thrive.

1 Thessalonians 5:11 reminds us of the importance of encouraging one another and building each other up. This principle is essential within the family unit. Whether it's supporting your child's dreams, encouraging your spouse in their personal development, or helping a sibling through a challenge, your words and actions can make a profound difference.

There's a powerful quote that resonates deeply with this concept: "If there is no enemy within, the enemy outside can do us no harm." When our family stands united, with no internal conflicts or discouragement, we become resilient against external challenges. By nurturing a spirit of mutual encouragement and support, we strengthen our family from within, making it a safe haven where each member can grow without fear or doubt.

As a family, it's important to recognize and celebrate each other's goals and achievements, no matter how big or small. By doing so, you create a positive and uplifting atmosphere where growth is nurtured, and each member feels valued and supported. This doesn't just strengthen individual members—it fortifies the entire family, creating a legacy of love, encouragement, and mutual respect.

Prayer

Heavenly Father, thank You for the gift of family and the opportunity to encourage and support one another. Help us to be intentional in our efforts to build each other up, creating an environment where everyone feels valued, loved, and encouraged to grow.

Lord, guide us in recognizing the unique gifts and goals You have placed in each family member. Give us the wisdom and compassion to support one another with words and actions that reflect Your love. Help us to celebrate each milestone and achievement, knowing that these moments contribute to the growth and unity of our family.

In Jesus' name, Amen.

Faith in Action – Supporting Each Other's Growth

Today, I commit to celebrating the goals and achievements of my family members. I will take the time to acknowledge their efforts, offer words of encouragement, and find meaningful ways to support their growth. May our family be a source of strength and love for each other, reflecting Your grace in all we do

———————————————————————————

———————————————————————————

———————————————————————————

———————————————————————————

———————————————————————————

Healing Family Wounds

Therefore, as God's chosen people, holy and dearly loved, clothe yourselves with compassion, kindness, humility, gentleness, and patience. Bear with each other and forgive one another if any of you has a grievance against someone. Forgive as the Lord forgave you. And over all these virtues put on love, which binds them all together in perfect unity."
— Colossians 3:12-14

The loss of a partner and the transition from a two-parent home to a single-parent household can leave deep emotional wounds within a family. These wounds may manifest as pain, anger, or resentment, making it difficult to move forward in love and unity. Yet, the scripture from Colossians calls us to clothe ourselves with compassion, kindness, humility, gentleness, and patience—even in the most challenging times.

In the aftermath of such loss, it's essential to seek and offer forgiveness within the family. Healing begins when we choose to forgive, not only for the sake of others but for our own peace and well-being. This doesn't mean that the pain disappears, but it does mean that we release the grip that hurt has on our hearts, making room for God's healing love to take its place.

Forgiveness within the family can be particularly challenging because the wounds often run deep, and the loss of a partner or the change in family structure can trigger feelings of betrayal, abandonment, or failure. However, by embracing the virtues outlined in Colossians, we can begin to mend these broken relationships. Compassion allows us to understand each other's pain, kindness helps us to extend grace, and humility reminds us that we all need forgiveness.

Prayer

Heavenly Father, I come before You today with a heavy heart, acknowledging the wounds that my family has endured. The loss of a partner and the transition from a two-parent home have left scars that only You can heal. I ask for Your grace and strength as we navigate these difficult emotions and seek to forgive one another.

Lord, help us to clothe ourselves with the virtues You've outlined in Your Word. May we approach each other with compassion, kindness, humility, gentleness, and patience. Teach us to bear with one another and to forgive as You have forgiven us. Let Your love be the bond that brings our family back together in unity.

In Jesus' name, Amen.

Faith in Action - Healing Family Wounds

As you reflect on the hurts that have affected your family, consider how you might take the first step toward healing. It may involve initiating a difficult conversation, acknowledging past mistakes, or simply offering a sincere apology.

DAY 58

Celebrating Family Milestones

"To everything there is a season, a time for every purpose under heaven."
— **Ecclesiastes 3:1**

Life is made up of seasons, each with its own purpose and significance. In the midst of our daily routines and responsibilities, it's easy to overlook the importance of pausing to celebrate the milestones that mark our journey. Yet, these moments—birthdays, graduations, anniversaries, and other significant events— are opportunities to honor God's faithfulness and the growth He has brought into our lives.

Ecclesiastes 3:1 reminds us that there is a time for everything, including a time to celebrate. Family milestones are not just about reaching a particular date or achieving a specific goal; they are about recognizing the ways in which God has been at work in our lives. Celebrating these moments allows us to express gratitude, deepen our connections with loved ones, and create lasting memories that will be cherished for years to come.

Honoring family milestones is also a way to reinforce the values and traditions that are important to your family. It's a time to come together, to reflect on where you've been, and to look forward with hope and anticipation for what God will do next. Whether the milestone is big or small, taking the time to celebrate it with intention can bring joy, unity, and a renewed sense of purpose to your family.

As you reflect on the milestones in your family's life, consider how you can make the upcoming ones even more meaningful. Whether it's planning a special dinner, organizing a gathering, or simply taking a moment to pray and give thanks, these celebrations are a way to honor God's presence in your journey and to strengthen the bonds that hold your family together.

Prayer

Heavenly Father, thank You for the seasons of life and for the milestones that remind us of Your faithfulness. As we celebrate these important moments, help us to do so with hearts full of gratitude and joy. May our celebrations honor You and bring our family closer together.

Lord, guide me as I plan for the upcoming milestones in our family. Give me the wisdom to create meaningful celebrations that reflect our love for each other and our trust in You. Help us to see these moments as opportunities to build lasting memories and to reinforce the values that are important to us.

In Jesus' name, Amen

Faith in Action - Celebrating Family Milestones

Today, I commit to planning a celebration for an upcoming family milestone. I will take the time to reflect on the significance of this moment and to honor it in a way that brings glory to You and joy to our family.

Creating New Family Faith Traditions

These commandments that I give you today are to be on your hearts.
Impress them on your children. Talk about them when you sit at home and
when you walk along the road, when you lie down and when you get up."
— Deuteronomy 6:6-7

Family traditions are the threads that weave the fabric of our lives together, creating a sense of continuity, belonging, and shared identity. For families who have experienced significant change, like a divorce, the establishment of new traditions can be a powerful way to reaffirm your faith, strengthen your bonds, and create a new sense of normalcy.

Deuteronomy 6:6-7 speaks to the importance of embedding God's Word into the daily rhythms of our lives. It encourages us to intentionally pass down our faith to the next generation, making it a living, breathing part of our family's culture. Creating new family faith traditions is one way to do this. These traditions—whether they are daily prayers, weekly Bible studies, or special holiday celebrations—serve as a constant reminder of God's presence and faithfulness in your lives.

As you reflect on the importance of family traditions, think about the practices that have been meaningful in your past, as well as new ones that could be meaningful for your family now. What faith-centered activities can you introduce that will help your family connect with God and with each other? Remember, these traditions don't have to be elaborate; their value lies in the consistency and intention behind them.

Establishing new traditions provides an opportunity to create fresh memories and reinforce your family's commitment to following God. As you move forward, consider how these practices can shape your family's faith journey, bringing you closer to God and to one another.

Prayer

Heavenly Father, thank You for the gift of family and the opportunity to create new traditions that honor You. I pray for Your guidance as we seek to establish practices that will deepen our faith and strengthen our bonds. Help us to be intentional in the ways we pass down our faith to the next generation, ensuring that Your Word is always at the center of our lives.

Lord, as we embark on this journey of creating new family faith traditions, I ask for Your blessing and wisdom. Show us how to incorporate these practices into our daily lives in ways that are meaningful and lasting. May these traditions bring us closer to You and to one another, fostering a spirit of love, unity, and devotion.

In Jesus' name, Amen.

Faith in Action – Creating New Family Faith Traditions

What new faith tradition can you establish to help your family grow closer to God and one another? Reflect on how this practice can serve as a reminder of God's love and faithfulness in your lives. Write down one step you'll take today to make this tradition a reality.

Reflect and Recharge as a Parent Leader After Divorce

As you come to the end of this 60-day journey, it's essential to take a moment to reflect on the path you've traveled, especially in your role as a parent leader after divorce. These past weeks have likely been filled with challenges, growth, and new insights as you've navigated your responsibilities and sought to rebuild your family on a foundation of faith and love.

At Leaders Wellness Suite, we understand that divorce brings about significant changes, not only in your personal life but also in how you lead and nurture your family. Throughout this journey, you've been intentional about focusing on your well-being, strengthening family bonds, and establishing a new normal for your household. Reflect on the personal growth you've experienced as a parent leader. How have you adapted to this new season of life? What victories have you achieved, and how has your relationship with your children evolved?

This period of reflection is also an opportunity to acknowledge the areas where you may still need to grow. Parenting after divorce requires resilience, wisdom, and a deep reliance on God's guidance. Consider the lessons you've learned and the insights you've gained over these 60 days. How can you carry these forward as you continue to lead your family with grace and strength?

Remember, this journey is ongoing. As you look back, also look forward with hope and determination. Your role as a parent leader is vital, and God is with you every step of the way, providing the strength and wisdom you need to guide your family through this season and beyond.

Prayer

Heavenly Father, I thank You for Your guidance throughout these past 60 days. As I reflect on this journey, I see the growth and progress You've enabled me to achieve as a parent leader after divorce. Thank You for the strength and wisdom You've provided as I've sought to rebuild my family on a foundation of faith and love.

Lord, as I move forward, I ask for Your continued presence and guidance. Help me to set new goals that will not only benefit me but also support the well-being of my children and our family as a whole. Give me the wisdom to lead with compassion, patience, and grace.

In Jesus' name, Amen.

Reflect & Recharge as a Parent Leader After Divorce

Today, I commit to reflecting on the lessons I've learned and setting new goals for the next phase of our journey. I will seek Your wisdom in every decision and trust that You will continue to lead us on the path of healing and growth. May our family continue to grow stronger in love and unity, reflecting Your grace in all we do.

____

____

____

____

____

This Week's Goals

Specific — What am I led to accomplish and why?

Measurable — How will I know when I have accomplished it?

Achievable — How can I accomplish this goal?

Relevant — Is this the right time for me to be working towards this goal?

Timebound — When do I want to accomplish this goal by?

☑ *Goal 1*

____

____

____

____

☑ *Goal 2*

____

____

____

____

☑ *Goal 3*

____

____

____

____

Conclusion

At Leaders Wellness Suite, we believe that reflecting on your journey allows you to recharge and set your sights on what lies ahead. This time of reflection is not just about looking back but about setting the stage for continued growth and healing. Embrace this moment to recharge your spirit and set new goals that will guide your family towards a future filled with hope, strength, and God's unending love.

Prayer of Salvation

Heavenly Father,

I come to You today, admitting my need for Your grace. I believe that You sent Your Son, Jesus Christ, to die for my sins and that He rose again, offering me new life. I repent of my sins and ask for Your forgiveness.

Lord Jesus, I invite You into my heart as my Savior and Lord. Lead me and guide me in Your ways.

Holy Spirit, fill me with Your presence and power. Help me to walk in faith, love, and obedience, living a life that glorifies You.

Thank You, Father, for Your unconditional love. Thank You, Jesus, for saving me. And thank You, Holy Spirit, for living in me. I am Yours forever.

In Jesus' name, Amen.

Additional Insights

Acknowledgments

This book would not have been possible without the contributions and support of many talented individuals. Your creativity and precision have brought this book to life visually and structurally—I deeply appreciate your work. To my family and friends, your encouragement and prayers have been my source of strength throughout this journey. To my mentors and colleagues, thank you for your guidance and inspiration along the way. Above all, I give thanks to God for His wisdom, grace, and provision in this process. Each of you has played a vital role in bringing this book to fruition, and I am truly grateful.

About the Author

Christy Copeland is the founder of Leaders Wellness Suite, a faith-based personal growth company dedicated to supporting families who have experienced trauma. As a mother of four, she understands firsthand the challenges of parenting after loss and trauma. With over 25 years of experience in business leadership and a background in behavioral science and legal studies, she brings a unique blend of personal experience and professional expertise to her work. Christy is the author of "Triumph After Trauma: 11 Keys to Positive Parenting After Trauma" and a certified transformation coach since 2017. She specializes in wellness, relationship building, parenting, and advocacy preparation. Her compassionate and faith-driven approach has helped countless families find hope and resilience.

Connect With Us

This 60-day journey may be complete, but it's only the beginning of what God has in store for you. At Leaders Wellness Suite, we're passionate about walking alongside families like yours as you heal, grow, and thrive.

I'd love to invite you to join our online community, where you can share your story, find encouragement, and connect with others who are on similar paths. Your journey and insights could be a blessing to someone else who's seeking hope and direction. Together, we'll continue building a foundation of faith, love, and resilience.

If Kingdom Musings has encouraged or inspired you, would you consider sharing your experience by leaving a review? Your feedback not only helps us serve families better but also allows others to discover the resources they need for their journey.

Visit www.leaderswellnesssuite.com to join the community, explore additional resources, or share your thoughts. Let's keep growing together, one step at a time.

With love and blessings,

Coach Christy

www.ingramcontent.com/pod-product-compliance
Lightning Source LLC
Chambersburg PA
CBHW080358030726

47598CB00010B/2801